Table of Contents

Capitalization

Sentences

Introduction

This book is designed to help students have a better understanding of grammar, the fundamental organizing principle of language. The standards for most states as well as the Common Core State Standards require that students "Demonstrate command of the conventions of standard English grammar usage when writing and speaking." Students who understand how to use proper grammar are better able to say what they mean when writing and speaking.

Each of the 64 worksheets in this book reinforces a grade-appropriate grammar topic. The book is organized by parts of speech and other key topics. The goal is to equip students with an understanding of grammar so they can communicate more effectively.

How to Use This Book

Here are just a few of the many ways you can use this book.

Grammar Mini-Lessons: The most basic way to use this book is as a source of grammar mini-lessons. Write the grammar rule on the board. You can copy this straight from the gray box found on each worksheet. Introduce the rule, explain it, and then give examples. See if students can come up with their own examples. Then have students complete the worksheet. You can ask students to complete the worksheets individually or with partners, depending on ability levels. Check for understanding.

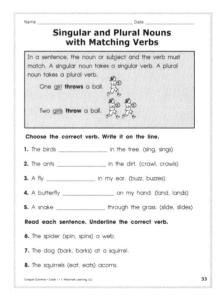

Grammar Reinforcement: After you have taught students a particular grammar rule, you can use these worksheets to give students the practice they need to reinforce their knowledge of the skill.

Grammar Assessment: The worksheets can serve as a formative assessment tool to show you where students might need additional teaching. Worksheets can also serve as a final assessment to confirm that students have mastered a particular rule.

Beyond the Book

There are myriad ways in which you can extend the lessons in this book. The goal is to keep the learning fun and interactive. Here are several ideas to get you started.

- Find examples of grammar rules you are studying in books you are reading in class. Point out these examples to students. Then send students on a grammar-rule scavenger hunt to find examples themselves. You can expand the search area to books students read at home and in magazines, newspapers, notices around school, advertisements—anywhere there are written words. The more places students see the rule being used, the better.

- Ask students to practice using specific grammar rules in their own writing. For example, if you are studying a particular type of punctuation, have students use that punctuation in their writing. They can even go back and revise old work using knowledge gained from learning new grammar rules.

- Create a short daily exercise in which students are asked to use a recently learned grammar rule to correct a sentence that is written on the board. Students love correcting others' mistakes!

Key Tips for Teaching English Learners

The rules of grammar vary between languages. This can make learning English grammar particularly difficult for English Learners. It is helpful to know where the grammar rules between languages differ enough to cause a fair amount of confusion. Here are some of those areas.

Word Order	In languages such as Spanish, Farsi, Arabic, and Korean, word order in sentences may vary from that of English.
Verbs	In English, verbs are inflected for person and number. (*Everyone cooks food. She has a large cat.*) Verbs are not inflected for person and number in Vietnamese, Hmong, Korean, Cantonese, and Mandarin. (*Everyone cook food. She have large cat.*)
Nouns	Nouns and adjectives use different forms in English. (*They felt safe in their home. They were concerned about safety.*) In Spanish, Hmong, Cantonese, and Mandarin, speakers use the same form for nouns and adjectives. (*They felt safety in their home.*)
Possessive Nouns	In English, we add an apostrophe and *s* to most singular nouns, or an apostrophe only to proper, plural names that end in *s*, to show possession. In Spanish, Vietnamese, Hmong, and Tagalog, possession is shown using *of*. It is always *of Holly*, not *Holly's*.
Plural Nouns	Nouns become plural after a number greater than one in English. (*We go home in two weeks. They are bringing five shirts.*) In Vietnamese, Hmong, Tagalog, Korean, Cantonese, Mandarin, and Farsi, there is no change in the noun following a number. (*We go home in two week. They are bringing five shirt.*)
Adjectives	Adjectives precede the nouns they modify in English (*the blue flower*). In Spanish, Vietnamese, Hmong, Farsi, and Arabic, adjectives follow the nouns they modify (*the flower blue*).
Pronouns	In English, there is a distinction between subject and object pronouns. (*He gave it to me. We spent time with her.*) In Spanish, Vietnamese, Hmong, Cantonese, Mandarin, and Farsi, there is no distinction. (*He gave it to I. We spent time with she.*)
Prepositions	The use of prepositions in other languages differs from those used in English. (English: *The movie is on the DVD.* Spanish: *The movie is in the DVD.*)
Articles	Indefinite articles are used consistently in English. (*She is a brilliant scientist. He is an electrician.*) In Spanish, Hmong, Tagalog, Cantonese, and Mandarin, indefinite articles can be omitted. (*She is brilliant scientist. He is electrician.*)

Common and Proper Nouns

A common noun names any person, place, or thing.
A proper noun names a specific person, place, or thing.
Each main word in a proper noun should begin with a
capital letter.

Common Noun	Proper Noun
friend	Sophie
ocean	Pacific
day	Monday

Read each sentence. Write the proper noun on the line.

1. Mrs. Ortiz lived near an empty lot. _____

2. Last Saturday, she planted a garden. _____

3. Her friends on Main Street helped. _____

4. Sophie weeded. _____

5. Julian planted seeds. _____

6. By April, flowers had sprouted. _____

7. By May, all the flowers had bloomed. _____

8. Juan likes to play in the garden. _____

Common and Proper Nouns

A common noun names any person, place, or thing.
A proper noun names specific person, place, or thing.
Each main word in a proper noun should begin with a capital letter.

Common Noun	Proper Noun
girl	Lucy
city	Dallas
country	United States

Draw a line under the proper noun in each sentence.

1. My favorite team is the Red Sox.

2. They play in Boston.

3. They won the World Series Championships eight times!

Choose a proper noun from the box to complete each sentence. Write it on the line.

San Diego Zoo   California   Vanessa

4. _____ and I love zoos!

5. There are lots of zoos in _____.

6. We will visit the _____ next.

Common and Proper Nouns

A common noun names any person, place, or thing.
A proper noun names a specific person, place, or thing.
Each main word in a proper noun should begin with a capital letter.

Common Noun: The **girl** has a kitten.

Proper Noun: Kate has a kitten.

Circle the proper noun in each sentence. Write it correctly on the line.

1. samantha hopes to win the game. _____

2. He visited new york. _____

3. There is a concert this saturday. _____

4. My friend maria is funny. _____

5. The family moved here from arizona. _____

6. The team meets every friday. _____

7. My aunt lives in california. _____

8. I like the cold weather in alaska. _____

Conquer Grammar • Grade 1 • © Newmark Learning, LLC

Common and Proper Nouns

A common noun names any person, place, or thing.
A proper noun names specific person, place, or thing.
Each main word in a proper noun should begin with a
capital letter.

People	Places	Things
Anna	Cleveland	Lake Erie
Nana	Africa	White House

Underline the proper noun in each sentence.
Then write it correctly on the line.

1. I live in brooklyn. _____

2. I have a twin brother, nate. _____

3. We play in prospect park. _____

4. We walk over the brooklyn bridge. _____

Rewrite each sentence with correct capitalization.

5. We like to eat in chinatown.

_____

6. Our favorite restaurant is red lotus.

_____

Name _____ Date _____

Common and Proper Nouns

A common noun names a person, place, or thing.
A proper noun names a specific person, place, or thing.
Each main word in a proper noun should begin with a capital letter.

Common Noun: My **aunt** works at a college.

Proper Nouns: **Aunt Carol** works at **Michigan State University**.

Circle the proper noun in each sentence.
Write it correctly on the line.

1. I am visiting france. _____

2. glenn created a sculpture for our school.

_____

3. My friends live in los angeles. _____

4. My whole family plays a game of football on thanksgiving.

_____

5. Winter starts in december. _____

6. carlos likes apples. _____

7. We have a barbecue every independence day.

_____

 Conquer Grammar • Grade 1 • © Newmark Learning, LLC

Singular and Plural Nouns

Singular nouns tell about one person, place, or thing. Plural nouns tell about more than one person, place, or thing. Add **s** to the end of most nouns to make them plural. For nouns ending in **x**, **z**, **s**, **sh**, or **ch**, add **es**. For nouns ending in a consonant and **y**, change the **y** to **i** and add **es**.

one cat	two **cats**
one fox	three **foxes**
one puppy	two **puppies**

Look at the picture. Write the noun that goes with the picture.

1. _____

2.  _____

3.  _____

4.  _____

5. _____

6.   _____

Possessive Nouns

Possessive nouns show that a person, place, or thing has or owns something. Add an apostrophe ' and an **s** to turn most singular nouns into possessive nouns.

The <u>coat of the girl</u> is warm.

The **girl's** coat is warm.

Write a possessive noun for each sentence.

1. _____ basket has snacks.
   Dad

2. _____ basket has sandwiches.
   Mom

3. The _____ windows are open.
   car

4. The _____ breeze is cool.
   day

5. The _____ water is blue.
   lake

6. The _____ bathing suit is colorful.
   boy

Possessive Nouns

Possessive nouns show that a person, place, or thing has or owns something. Add an apostrophe ' and an **s** to turn most singular nouns into possessive nouns.

The <u>door of the school</u> is open.

The **school's** door is open.

Write a possessive noun for each sentence.

1. The _____ bark is loud.
dog

2. My _____ bike is blue.
brother

3. _____ eyes are brown.
Sam

4. The _____ fur is fluffy.
cat

5. The _____ nest is empty.
bird

6. The _____ ears are floppy.
dog

Possessive Nouns

Possessive nouns show that a person, place, or thing has or owns something. Add an apostrophe ' and an **s** to turn most singular nouns into possessive nouns.

The <u>park of the town</u> is big.

The **town's** park is big.

Write the possessive phrase for the underlined words.

1. The <u>wing of the bird</u> is red. _____

2. The <u>skin of the baby</u> is soft. _____

3. Where is <u>the key of Paul</u>? _____

4. We washed <u>the car of Dad</u>. _____

5. The <u>bowl of the dog</u> is broken. _____

6. <u>The hat of Kate</u> is lost. _____

7. The <u>window of the car</u> is open. _____

8. Please walk the <u>dog of the neighbor</u>. _____

Singular and Plural Verbs

Add **s** to the end of most verbs to make them singular. For verbs ending in **x**, **z**, **s**, **sh**, or **ch**, add **es**. For verbs ending in a consonant and **y**, change the **y** to **i** and add **es**. Do not add **s** to the end of a plural verb.

Singular Verb	Plural Verb
The tiger **roars**.	The tigers **roar**.
The girl **fixes** the bike.	The girls **fix** the bike.
The hamster **scurries**.	The hamsters **scurry**.

Read each sentence. Underline the correct verb.

1. Jorge and Dad (drive, drives) to the lake.

2. The sun (shine, shines) in the sky.

3. Jorge (try, tries).

4. Dad (help, helps) him.

5. Jorge (learn, learns) fast.

Choose the correct verb. Write it on the line.

6. They _____. (watch, watches)

7. Jorge _____ on a star. (wish, wishes)

Singular and Plural Verbs

Singular verbs tell about the action of one person, place, or thing. Plural verbs tell about the action of more than one person, place, or thing. Add **s** to the end of most verbs to make them singular. A plural verb should not end in **s**.

One cat **sleeps**.

Two cats **sleep**.

Choose the correct verb. Write it on the line.

1. The bees _____ for honey. (look, looks)

2. The bird _____ berries. (find, finds)

3. The rabbit _____ grass. (eat, eats)

4. The squirrels _____ for nuts. (hunt, hunts)

5. The foxes _____ their food. (hide, hides)

6. The sun _____. (set, sets)

7. The animals _____. (sleep, sleeps)

8. The stars _____. (shine, shines)

Present Tense Verbs

Verbs are action words. Present tense verbs tell about actions that are happening right now. For the present tense, add **-s** or **-es** if the subject of a sentence is singular. Do not add **-s** or **-es** if the subject is plural.

Fred **likes** the color yellow.

Cara and Raul **like** the movie.

Write the present tense form of the verb in the parentheses ( ).

1. Davis (play) soccer. _____

2. Marta and Pat (answer) questions. _____

3. Dad (call) to us. _____

4. The players (run) around the field. _____

5. Connor (eat) the sandwich. _____

6. Grandma (drive) us. _____

Present Tense Verbs

Verbs are action words. Present tense verbs tell about actions that are happening right now. For the present tense, add **-s** or **-es** if the subject of a sentence is singular. Do not add **-s** or **-es** if the subject is plural.

Sam **plays** soccer on Saturdays.

Billy and Mia **play** tag.

Write the present tense form of the verb in the parentheses ( ).

1. Lisa, José, and Vinny (build) a fort._____

2. They (use) branches. _____

3. Vinny (ask) Mom for a sheet. _____

4. Mom (give) him a sheet. _____

5. They (finish) the fort. _____

6. Mom (bring) them a snack. _____

Present Tense Verbs

Verbs are action words. Present tense verbs tell about actions that are happening right now. For the present tense, add **-s** or **-es** if the subject of a sentence is singular. Do not add **-s** or **-es** if the subject is plural.

Rose **runs** around the house.

Lisa and Austin **run** around the tree.

Write the present tense form of the verb in the parentheses ( ).

1. Ed and Robbie (play) catch. _____

2. The dog (watch) them. _____

3. Ed (toss) the ball. _____

4. Robbie (miss) the ball. _____

5. The dog (catch) it! _____

6. Ed and Robbie (laugh). _____

Past Tense Verbs

Past tense verbs tell about actions that already happened. Past tense verbs often end in **-ed**.

He **looked** both ways.

He **crossed** the street.

Write the past tense form of the verb in the parentheses ( ).

1. We (look) at the sky. _____

2. We (learn) about stars. _____

3. I (help) Matt see. _____

4. The sun (warm) Sara's face. _____

5. The clouds (block) the sun. _____

6. It (start) to rain. _____

7. I (listen) to music for an hour. _____

Past Tense Verbs

Past tense verbs tell about actions that already happened. Past tense verbs often end in **-ed**.

We **jumped** high.

We **reached** for the stars.

Write the past tense form of the verb.

1. We _____ home from school.
    walk

2. Liam and I _____ in the yard.
    play

3. We _____ the tree.
    climb

4. Mom _____ us inside.
    call

5. We all _____ Mom cook dinner.
    help

6. Mom _____ me to set the table.
    ask

Irregular Past Tense Verbs

Past tense verbs tell about actions that already happened. Past tense verbs that do not end in **-ed** are irregular. Some examples of verbs and their irregular past tense forms include **break/broke, wear/wore, know/knew, teach/taught.**

Pablo **broke** the glass.

Kim **wore** a red cap.

Tom **drew** a picture.

Underline the verb in each sentence. Then write the past tense form of the verb.

1. I know the answer. _____

2. School begin last month. _____

3. Amy know where to look for the cat. _____

4. Richard break the vase. _____

5. Rita wear her new shoes. _____

6. She teach the class. _____

Future Tense Verbs

Future tense verbs tell about actions that will happen at a later time. To form the future tense, place the word **will** in front of the verb.

Birds **will build** nests in the spring.

Mom **will plant** tomatoes in June.

Write the future tense form of the verb in the parentheses ( ).

1. I (make) the team. _____

2. I (practice) every day. _____

3. Dad (teach) me to hit. _____

4. We (toss) the ball. _____

5. Mom (run) with me. _____

6. I (play) baseball. _____

Future Tense Verbs

Future tense verbs tell about actions that will happen at a later time. To form the future tense, place the word **will** in front of the verb.

Tomorrow, we **will go** to the library.

I **will do** my homework after school.

Write the future tense form of the verb in the parentheses ( ).

1. I (be) an astronaut one day. _____

2. I (wear) a space suit. _____

3. I (fly) the space ship. _____

4. My ship (land) on Mars. _____

5. My family (miss) me. _____

6. We (talk) using computers. _____

Verb Tenses

The tense of a verb shows when the action happens. To form the past tense of most verbs, add **-ed**. For the present tense, either use the verb as is or add **-s** or **-es**. To form the future tense, place the word **will** in front of the verb.

Past:
Last month, Jonah **played** golf.

Present:
Today, Jonah **plays** hockey.

Future:
Next week, Jonah **will play** soccer.

Read each sentence. Write *present, past,* or *future* for the underlined verb.

1. Last year, we moved here. _____

2. I started a new school. _____

3. We adopted a dog. _____

4. I walk the dog to the park. _____

5. I will play with the dog after school every day.

_____

Choose the correct verb. Write it on the line.

6. Last week, I _____ my cousins. (called, will call)

7. Next week, we _____ them. (visited, will visit)

Verb Tenses

The tense of a verb shows when the action happens. To form the past tense of most verbs, add **-ed**. For the present tense, either use the verb as is or add **-s** or **-es**. To form the future tense, place the word **will** in front of the verb.

Past:
Last week, Alex **cleaned** the hamster cage.

Present:
This week, I **clean** the hamster cage.

Future:
Next week, Jane **will clean** the hamster cage.

Read each sentence. Write *present*, *past*, or *future* for the underlined verb.

1. Yesterday, I walked home from school. _____

2. I talked with my best friends. _____

3. I will walk home if the sun is out. _____

4. Dad will drive me on rainy days. _____

5. I like to walk. _____

**Complete each sentence with one of the following verbs:
*played, will play, play.***

6. Next month, we _____ soccer.

7. Last month, we _____ basketball.

Verb Tenses

The tense of a verb shows when the action happens. To form the past tense of most verbs, add **-ed**. For the present tense, either use the verb as is or add **-s** or **-es**. To form the future tense, place the word **will** in front of the verb.

Past:
Yesterday, we **visited** a museum.

Present:
Now, we **visit** a zoo.

Future:
Tomorrow, we **will visit** a water park.

Read each sentence. Write *present*, *past*, or *future* for the underlined verb.

1. Last year, we painted my room. _____

2. Next spring, I will play baseball. _____

3. Ella kicks the ball. _____

4. We discovered a raccoon. _____

5. Mr. Jones will speak on Monday. _____

Choose the correct verb. Write it on the line.

6. Last winter, we _____ to Florida. (travel, traveled)

7. Suzy _____ the dog now. (walked, walks)

Verb Tenses

The tense of a verb shows when the action happens.
To form the past tense of most verbs, add **-ed**. For the present tense, either use the verb as is or add **-s** or **-es**.
To form the future tense, place the word **will** in front of the verb.

Past:
Last year, Jenna **danced** ballet.

Present:
This year, Jenna **dances** jazz.

Future:
Next year, Jenna **will dance** hip-hop.

Choose the correct verb. Write it on the line.

1. Tomorrow, we _____ muffins. (baked, will bake)

2. Last week, we _____ about trees. (learn, learned)

3. Arlo _____ the ball now. (tossed, tosses)

4. This morning, Mr. Bensz _____ eggs. (cook, cooked)

5. The leaves _____ color in the fall.
(will change, changed)

Read each sentence. Write *present*, *past*, or *future* for the underlined verb.

6. After practice, Jordan <u>rubbed</u> her legs. _____

7. I <u>like</u> animals. _____

Singular Nouns with Matching Verbs

A singular noun names one person, place, or thing. In a sentence, the noun or subject and the verb must match. A singular noun takes a singular verb. Singular verbs end in **-s** or **-es**.

The <u>girl</u> **cooks** rice.

The <u>boy</u> **bakes** a cake.

Write the singular form of the verb to match the singular noun.

1. Justin _____ across the street.

     look

2. Milu _____ next to him.

    stand

3. A friend _____ to them.

     wave

4. The sun _____ to set.

     start

5. Mom _____ Justin and Milu.

     call

6. She _____ help with dinner.

    need

Plural Nouns with Matching Verbs

A plural noun names more than one person, place, or thing. In a sentence, the noun or subject and the verb must match. A plural noun takes a plural verb. Plural verbs do not end in **-s**.

The <u>kids</u> **walk** down the street.

<u>Tim and Mia</u> **run** around the track.

Read each sentence. Underline the correct verb.

1. The dogs (chase, chases) the cats.

2. The boys (wash, washes) the car.

3. The teachers (reads, read) the directions.

4. The students (writes, write) their names.

5. The swans (glide, glides) across the pond.

Choose the correct verb. Write it on the line.

6. The babies _____. (nap, naps)

7. The toddlers _____. (plays, play)

8. The girls _____. (skip, skips)

Singular and Plural Nouns with Matching Verbs

In a sentence, the noun or subject and the verb must match. A singular noun takes a singular verb. A plural noun takes a plural verb.

One <u>girl</u> **throws** a ball.

Two <u>girls</u> **throw** a ball.

Choose the correct verb. Write it on the line.

1. The birds _____ in the tree. (sing, sings)

2. The ants _____ in the dirt. (crawl, crawls)

3. A fly _____ in my ear. (buzz, buzzes)

4. A butterfly _____ on my hand. (land, lands)

5. A snake _____ through the grass. (slide, slides)

Read each sentence. Underline the correct verb.

6. The spider (spin, spins) a web.

7. The dog (bark, barks) at a squirrel.

8. The squirrels (eat, eats) acorns.

Singular and Plural Nouns
with Matching Verbs

In a sentence, the noun or subject and the verb must match. A singular noun takes a singular verb. A plural noun takes a plural verb.

Singular: The <u>flower</u> **grows**.

Plural: The <u>flowers</u> **grow**.

Read each sentence. Underline the correct verb.

1. The baby (sleep, sleeps) in her crib.

2. Dad (feed, feeds) the baby.

3. Mom and Dad (play, plays) with the baby.

4. Mom and Dad (sing, sings) to the baby.

5. The baby (clap, claps).

Choose the correct verb. Write it on the line.

6. The baby _____. (watch, watches)

7. She _____ to sing. (start, starts)

8. The baby _____ quickly. (learn, learns)

 Conquer Grammar • Grade 1 • © Newmark Learning, LLC

Singular and Plural Nouns with Matching Verbs

In a sentence, the noun or subject and the verb must match. A singular noun takes a singular verb. A plural noun takes a plural verb.

Singular: The <u>frog</u> **jumps**.

Plural: The two <u>frogs</u> **jump**.

Read each sentence. Underline the correct verb.

1. My friends (walk, walks) to the garden.

2. Tina (plant, plants) seeds.

3. John (water, waters) the garden.

4. Fran and Molly (pull, pulls) out weeds.

5. Vegetables (grow, grows) in the spring.

Choose the correct verb. Write it on the line.

6. Our parents _____ cook the vegetables. (help, helps)

7. I _____ to grow my food! (like, likes)

Singular and Plural Nouns with Matching Verbs

In a sentence, the noun or subject and the verb must match. A singular noun takes a singular verb. A plural noun takes a plural verb.

One <u>lion</u> **roars**.

Two <u>lions</u> **roar**.

Choose the correct verb. Write it on the line.

1. The family _____ New York City. (visit, visits)

2. Dina _____ at the skyscrapers. (look, looks)

3. The family _____ the subway. (ride, rides)

4. Lucas and Estella _____ pictures. (take, takes)

Read each sentence. Underline the correct verb.

5. Good students (follow, follows) rules.

6. Rules (keep, keeps) us safe.

7. The teacher (lead, leads) the class.

8. The principal (speak, speaks) at the meeting.

 Conquer Grammar • Grade 1 • © Newmark Learning, LLC

Personal Pronouns

Pronouns are words that take the place of nouns.

I, **he**, **she**, **we**, **they**, and **them** are personal pronouns.
Personal pronouns can be used to avoid repetition
of the noun.

Noun	**Personal Pronoun**
Mary goes to camp.	**She** goes to camp.

**Write the personal pronoun *he, she, they, him,* or
them for the underlined word or words.**

1. <u>Julie</u> lives in the city. _____

2. <u>David</u> lives in the country. _____

3. Julie visits <u>David.</u> _____

4. <u>Julie and David</u> climb trees. _____

5. The cat follows <u>Julie and David</u>! _____

6. <u>Julie</u> loves to visit David. _____

7. <u>Julie and David</u> have lots of fun together. _____

Personal Pronouns

Pronouns are words that take the place of nouns.
I, **he**, **she**, **we**, **they**, and **them** are personal pronouns.
Personal pronouns can be used to avoid repetition
of the noun.

Noun	**Personal Pronoun**
James has a goldfish.	**He** has a goldfish.
Maggie and **Janel** painted the room.	**They** painted the room.

Choose the correct personal pronoun from the box to complete each sentence. Write it on the line.

He	She	I	They	It

1. I live in a house. _____ has a flat roof.

2. My name is Alina. _____ am eight years old.

3. Jorge lives across the street. _____ has a twin sister.

4. Martina is Jorge's sister. _____ and Jorge look alike.

5. I like to play with Jorge and Martina. _____ are
my friends.

 Conquer Grammar • Grade 1 • © Newmark Learning, LLC

Possessive Pronouns

Pronouns take the place of nouns. Possessive pronouns show ownership. **My**, **his**, **her**, **our**, and **their** are possessive pronouns.

  I drink **my** milk.

  Mom drinks **her** water.

Choose the correct possessive pronoun from the box to complete each sentence. Write it on the line.

my	his	her	our	their

1. Nora took _____ jacket.

2. Noah brought _____ bike.

3. I packed _____ backpack.

4. We ate _____ snacks.

5. They ate _____ apples.

6. I liked _____ banana.

Personal and Possessive Pronouns

Pronouns are words that take the place of nouns.
Personal pronouns refer to specific people, places, or
things. Possessive pronouns show ownership.

Personal	**Possessive**
Alex and Jan read a book.	The book is **theirs.**
He reads a book.	The book is **his**.

**Write the personal pronoun *he, she,* or *they* for the
underlined word or words.**

1. <u>Mia</u> gets a bowl. _____

2. <u>Dad</u> adds lettuce. _____

3. <u>Mia and Dad</u> make a salad. _____

**Write the possessive pronoun *their, her,* or *his* for the
underlined word or words.**

4. Mia adds <u>Mia's</u> carrots. _____

5. Dad adds <u>Dad's</u> dressing. _____

6. Mia and Dad eat <u>Mia and Dad's</u> salads. _____

Indefinite Pronouns

Pronouns are words that take the place of nouns.
Indefinite pronouns don't refer to a specific
person or thing.

Somebody broke the vase.

Nobody is in the room.

Read each sentence. Circle the indefinite pronoun.

1. Everyone went to the park.

2. Someone called me.

3. Did you forget something?

4. Nobody wanted to go home.

5. Did anyone lose a jacket?

**Choose the correct indefinite pronoun. Write it on
the line.**

6. Did _____ knock?   (someone, anything)

7. _____ is looking out the window.
(Nothing, Somebody)

Indefinite Pronouns

Pronouns are words that take the place of nouns.
Indefinite pronouns don't refer to a specific
person or thing.

Is **anybody** home?

Everyone must be out.

Read each sentence. Circle the indefinite pronoun.

1. Somebody lost a hat.

2. Everyone is smiling.

3. Do you want anything to eat?

4. Someone is missing.

5. Did anyone call Laurel?

Choose the correct indefinite pronoun. Write it on the line.

6. There is _____ in the box. (anything, nothing)

7. _____ knows the answer. (Nobody, Nothing)

8. Did you talk to _____? (anyone, something)

Adjectives

Adjectives are words that describe nouns. Adjectives give details about people, places, and things. They tell about size, color, number, and kind.

The **three** boys jumped.

The **young** girls hopped.

Choose an adjective from the box to complete each sentence. Write it on the line.

heavy	sharp	two	blue	big	soft

1. Kari wears her _____ shirt.

2. Steve ate _____ cookies.

3. That elephant is so _____!

4. Don't touch the _____ glass.

5. Is the backpack too _____ to lift?

6. Sue likes her _____ blanket.

Adjectives

Adjectives are words that describe nouns. Adjectives give details about people, places, and things. They tell about size, color, number, and kind.

Andy ate **ten** grapes.

Try some of the **delicious** pizza!

Choose an adjective from the box to complete each sentence. Write it on the line.

| green | cold | one | fuzzy | loud |

1. The _____ alarm hurts my ears.

2. Bees are _____ insects.

3. Dad bought me _____ sandwich.

4. Nathan has a _____ hat.

5. I drank the _____ water.

Adjectives

Adjectives are words that describe nouns. Adjectives give details about people, places, and things. They tell about size, color, number, and kind.

Tina's cat has **green** eyes.

Stand under the **tall** tree.

Underline the adjective in each sentence.

1. Brendan wanted a new toy.

2. It was a difficult choice.

3. He liked the red car.

4. He also liked a yellow truck.

5. He chose the faster car.

6. He paid with shiny coins.

7. The clerk put the toy into a paper bag.

8. Brendan left the store with a big smile on his face.

Adjectives

Adjectives are words that describe nouns. Adjectives give details about people, places, and things. They tell about size, color, number, and kind.

Six roses are in the **tall** vase.

Read each sentence. Underline the adjective. Then write the noun it describes.

1. Ed likes bright sneakers. _____

2. Mr. Sanchez read a scary story. _____

3. Janet ate a sweet apple. _____

4. What's in the brown box? _____

5. Rabbits are quiet pets. _____

6. Ms. Burke drives a fast car. _____

7. The dog has long fur. _____

  Conquer Grammar • Grade 1 • © Newmark Learning, LLC

Adjectives

Adjectives are words that describe nouns. Adjectives give details about people, places, and things. They tell about size, color, number, and kind.

The **big** library is in the **white** building.

Read each sentence. Underline the adjective.
Then write the noun it describes.

1. Most spiders have eight eyes. _____

2. The tiny ant ate a crumb. _____

3. The orange bug landed on me. _____

4. Don't touch the red ants. _____

5. I don't like big spiders. _____

6. I see a brown earthworm. _____

7. Look at the pretty butterfly. _____

Name _____ Date _____

Adverbs

Adverbs describe verbs. They give details about how, when, or where an action happens.

The actors spoke **clearly**.   They heard the story **before**.

I lost my pen **somewhere**.   We **quickly** ran to the store.

Read each sentence. Circle the verb and underline the adverb.

1. Sophia happily agreed to dance in the ballet.

2. The dancers practiced daily.

3. The dance company presented the ballet outdoors.

4. Sophia performed beautifully.

5. Her friends threw a party afterward.

Underline the adverb in each sentence. Then circle whether the adverb tells *how, when,* or *where.*

6. Flowers grow everywhere.   How   When   Where

7. Tom carefully picks them.   How   When   Where

8. Soon, he will put them into a vase.   How   When   Where

Conquer Grammar • Grade 1 • © Newmark Learning, LLC

Prayers

Prepositions

Prepositions connect two or more words in a sentence and show how they are related. Some prepositions show where something is. Others show where or when something happens.

Pat put the plate **on** the table.

We listen **during** story hour.

Read each sentence. Underline the preposition.

1. There is a giant tree in the park.

2. We sit under the tree.

3. Squirrels run on the branches.

4. The leaves turn red during fall.

5. Then they fall to the ground.

6. I love to run through the leaf piles.

7. The owl is in the tree.

8. I watch the owl with Mom.

Prepositions

Prepositions connect two or more words in a sentence and show how they are related. Some prepositions show where something is. Others show where or when something happens.

Look **beyond** the river.

There is a rainbow **in** the sky.

Read each sentence. Underline the preposition.

1. I live in this house.

2. My cousins live across the street.

3. We live on a quiet road.

4. The park is around the corner.

5. Our school is beyond the park.

6. The supermarket is on Main Street.

7. Look at that cat!

8. It is on the roof.

Prepositions

Prepositions connect two or more words in a sentence and show how they are related. Some prepositions show where something is. Others show where or when something happens.

We walk **on** the grass.

We swim **in** the lake.

Choose the correct preposition. Write it on the line.

1. My family is going hiking (on, in) Sunday. _____

2. My friend Bella is coming (with, by) us. _____

3. We are sleeping (in, at) cabins. _____

4. We will tell stories (by, from) the fire. _____

5. We will toast hot dogs (of, on) sticks. _____

6. We will sing (under, at) the stars. _____

7. I love being (in, from) the woods. _____

8. I will wrap a blanket (around, at) me. _____

Prepositions

Prepositions connect two or more words in a sentence and show how they are related. Some prepositions show where something is. Others show where or when something happens.

I look **for** my glasses.

They are **on** the nightstand.

Choose the correct preposition. Write it on the line.

1. I walk (for, to) school. _____

2. I walk (at, with) my friends. _____

3. We walk (by, for) the park. _____

4. We look (for, in) bugs. _____

5. We see ants (at, on) the ground. _____

6. I look (at, near) my watch. _____

7. It is (after, under) eight o'clock! _____

8. We hurry (around, to) school. _____

Prepositions

Prepositions connect two or more words in a sentence and show how they are related. Some prepositions show where something is. Others show where or when something happens.

The milk is **for** the cereal.

The cat purred **at** me.

Choose a preposition from the box to complete each sentence. Write it on the line.

at	for	in	on	through

1. The cup is _____ the table.

2. Meet me _____ 8:30 in the morning.

3. The flower is _____ my mother.

4. My sister is _____ middle school.

5. Manny walked _____ the garden.

6. I put the book _____ the desk.

7. Jacob arrived _____ the game first.

8. Lena wrote a poem _____ me.

Name _____ Date _____

Prepositions

Prepositions help connect two words in a sentence and show how they are related. Some prepositions tell where something is. Others tell when something happens.

Walk **toward** the corner.

The clue is **on** the tree.

Choose the correct preposition from the box to complete each sentence. Write it on the line. You can use a preposition more than once.

toward	about	in	across	for	on

1. I look at the house _____ the street.

2. I think _____ my best friend.

3. Lucy moved _____ the country.

4. I look _____ the sky.

5. The sun sets _____ the west.

6. Stars sparkle _____ the sky.

7. I wish _____ my friend back.

8. I call Lucy _____ the phone.

54

Conquer Grammar • Grade 1 • © Newmark Learning, LLC

Conjunctions

Conjunctions are linking words. They combine two short sentences into a longer sentence. **And, or, but, so,** and **because** are conjunctions.

I eat breakfast **and** then brush my teeth.

I get the bus **and** go to school.

Read each sentence. Underline the conjunction.
Write it on the line.

1. I was tired, so I went to bed. _____

2. Is the glass full or empty? _____

3. Jan likes fall, but she doesn't like winter. _____

4. We went hiking and took pictures. _____

5. I took a bath because I was dirty. _____

6. You can do your homework now or later. _____

7. The sky turned gray, and it began to rain. _____

Conjunctions

Conjunctions are linking words. They combine two short sentences into a longer sentence. **And, or, but, so,** and **because** are conjunctions.

I eat dinner, **and** then I wash the dishes.

I read **or** play a game.

Read each sentence. Underline the conjunction.
Write it on the line.

1. Cheetahs have spots, and they run fast. _____

2. Bears may look cute, but they are dangerous. _____

3. Elephants splash in the water because they love to swim.

_____

4. Zebras have stripes, and no two zebras have the

same pattern. _____

5. Snakes can be tiny or huge. _____

6. Lions nap during the day, so they can hunt for food

at night. _____

Conjunctions

Conjunctions are linking words. They combine two short sentences into a longer sentence. **And, or, but, so,** and **because** are conjunctions.

Lila can take art, **or** she can take music.

I want to visit Grandpa **because** I miss him.

Read each sentence. Choose the correct conjunction. Write it on the line.

1. Joel wants to swim, _____ it is raining.

(but, or)

2. Luke is tired _____ it is late.

(or, because)

3. We will go to the zoo, _____ we will see animals.

(and, but)

4. Alice loves to draw, _____ she will take art.

(but, so)

5. We can stay in, _____ we can go out.

(so, or)

Conjunctions

Conjunctions are linking words. They combine two short sentences into a longer sentence. **And, or, but, so,** and **because** are conjunctions.

I like to ride my bike **and** visit Grandma.

Use a conjunction from the box to combine each pair of sentences. Write the new sentence on the line.

because	so	and

1. The band has a drummer. The band has a piano player.

_____

2. The band played an old song. People wanted to

sing along.

_____

_____

3. The band stopped playing. The band could rest.

_____

4. The crowd cheered. The crowd asked for more songs.

_____

Conjunctions

Conjunctions are linking words. They combine two short sentences into a longer sentence. **And, or, but, so,** and **because** are conjunctions. Place a comma before the conjunction **but.**

The bush has green leaves. The bush has purple flowers.

The bush has green leaves, but purple flowers.

Combine each pair of sentences using the conjunction in the parentheses ( ). Write the new sentence on the line. Add a comma if necessary.

1. We were hot. We were sweaty. (and)

_____

2. We could go to the pool. We could go to the lake. (or)

_____

3. The pool is closer. We went to the pool. (so)

_____

4. I know how to swim. I stayed near Mom. (but)

_____

_____

Conjunctions

Conjunctions are linking words. They combine two short sentences into a longer sentence. **And, or, but, so,** and **because** are conjunctions. Place a comma before the conjunction **but.**

We can read a book **or** play outside.

Use a conjunction from the box to combine each pair of sentences. Write the compound sentence on the line.

and	but	so	or

1. Tiffany likes dogs. She does not like cats.

_____

2. Mom gave the baby a bottle. Mom gave the baby cereal.

_____

3. We will eat dinner. We will eat dessert.

_____

4. I can read my book. I can walk to the park.

_____

Articles

The words **a**, **an**, and **the** are articles. Use **the** to tell about an exact person, place, or thing. Use **a** or **an** to tell about any person, place, or thing. Use **a** before a consonant sound and **an** before a vowel sound.

Nolan is in **the** cafeteria.

He drinks **a** carton of milk.

He eats **an** orange.

Choose the correct article. Write it on the line.

1. I'm in (an, the) city! _____

2. I see (a, an) skyscraper. _____

3. I take (a, an) taxi. _____

4. I ride (a, an) elevator. _____

5. I walk down (an, the) main street. _____

6. I want to get (a, an) gift for Mom. _____

7. I go to (an, the) store on the corner. _____

8. I buy her (a, an) postcard. _____

Articles

> The words **a**, **an**, and **the** are articles. Use **the** to tell about an exact person, place, or thing. Use **a** or **an** to tell about any person, place, or thing. Use **a** before a consonant sound and **an** before a vowel sound.
>
> I look in **the** desk.
>
> There is **a** notebook.
>
> There is also **an** eraser.

Choose the correct article. Write it on the line.

1. We visit (an, the) animal farm. _____

2. Pigs roll in (a, the) mud. _____

3. A hen lays (a, an) egg. _____

4. Cows chew on (an, the) grass. _____

5. I take (a, an) picture. _____

6. Chickens hop along (a, the) fence. _____

7. Sheep jump on (a, the) grass. _____

8. We learn how to milk (a, an) cow. _____

 Conquer Grammar • Grade 1 • © Newmark Learning, LLC

Demonstratives

This, that, these, and **those** are demonstratives. Demonstratives tell about specific people, places, or things. Use **this** and **that** with singular nouns, and **these** and **those** with plural nouns.

This is my street. **That** house is mine.

These clothes go into my closet. **Those** clothes go into my dresser.

Read each sentence. Choose the correct demonstrative. Write it on the line.

1. (These, This) zoo is huge. _____

2. (That, Those) giraffe is tall. _____

3. (This, These) monkeys are loud. _____

4. (These, That) lion is sleeping. _____

5. (Those, That) group is having a picnic. _____

6. (That, Those) kids are playing tag. _____

7. I like to sit on (these, that) big rock. _____

8. Tigers climb (those, that) trees. _____

Articles and Demonstratives

The words **a**, **an**, and **the** are articles. **This**, **that**, **these**, and **those** are demonstratives. Use articles and demonstratives before nouns.

The soccer player kicked **the** ball.

She kicked **that** ball hard!

She got **a** goal.

**Choose the correct article or demonstrative.
Write it on the line.**

1. The dog chased (these, the) cat. _____

2. (These, Those) birds over there are pretty. _____

3. I will wear (this, these) pants today. _____

4. Use (this, these) marker to color your picture. _____

5. (A, That) girl is wearing green socks. _____

6. Please put (a, this) juice into the cabinet. _____

7. Lila broke (a, an) plate. _____

8. Tom brought his dog to (the, these) vet. _____

Commas in Series

Use a comma to separate three or more words in a series.

Tina likes baseball, soccer, and tennis.

Read each sentence. Write commas where needed.

1. Monkeys tigers and elephants live in the jungle.

2. The kitten has brown black and tan spots.

3. We can play tag hopscotch or hide-and-seek.

Rewrite each sentence using the correct punctuation.

4. Andy has blue pink and yellow markers.

_____

5. Jimmy can sing dance and juggle.

_____

6. Sam packed yogurt fruit and toast for lunch.

_____

Commas in Dates and Series

Use commas in dates and to separate three or more words in a series.

My birthday is Thursday, August 8, 2013.

Cows, pigs, and turkeys live on the farm.

Read each sentence. Write commas where needed.

1. Birds eat seeds fruit and insects.

2. My brother was born on Monday August 22 2011.

3. You can play with Janine Lisa and Matt.

Rewrite each sentence using correct punctuation.

4. Nana was born on Tuesday May 15 1956.

_____

5. Kim Lulu and Maddie live upstairs.

_____

6. Ava went to the mall the park and the store.

_____

Commas in Dates and Series

Use commas in dates and to separate three or more words in a series.

We moved on Friday, July 11, 2014.

My scarf has blue, red, and yellow stripes.

Read each sentence. Write commas where needed.

1. The new restaurant opened on Saturday April 2 2016.

2. The restaurant sells hamburgers milkshakes and fries.

3. It is open on Fridays Saturdays and Sundays.

Rewrite each sentence, using correct punctuation.

4. The tag sale is on Saturday June 3 2017.

_____

5. Jen Tim and Lee leave for camp the next day.

_____

6. They come home on Tuesday August 22 2017.

_____

Name _____ Date _____

End Marks

An end mark is the punctuation that comes at the end of a sentence.

Statements, or telling sentences, end in a period: **.**
Sentences that ask a question end in a question mark: **?**
Sentences that show strong feeling end in an exclamation mark: **!**

Nina is eight years old**.**   Where are you moving**?**
Hurry up**!**

Read each sentence. Write the correct end mark.

1. What is your phone number _____

2. A car has four wheels _____

3. Watch out _____

4. We tiptoed down the street _____

5. Who is with your teacher _____

6. Where are you going _____

7. I can't wait _____

8. Are you ready to go _____

    Conquer Grammar • Grade 1 • © Newmark Learning, LLC

End Marks

An end mark is the punctuation that comes at the end of a sentence.

Statements, or telling sentences, end in a period: **.**
Sentences that ask a question end in a question mark: **?**
Sentences that show strong feeling end in an exclamation mark: **!**

I am tired**.** What time is it**?** It is late**!**

Read each sentence. Write the correct end mark.

1. My name is Charlie _____

2. What is your name _____

3. I live on Broom Street _____

4. Where do you live _____

5. I can't believe we are neighbors _____

Rewrite each sentence with the correct end mark.

6. I can't wait to bake

_____

7. What should we make

_____

End Marks

An end mark is the punctuation that comes at the end of a sentence.

Statements, or telling sentences, end in a period: **.**
Sentences that ask a question end in a question mark: **?**
Sentences that show strong feeling end in an exclamation mark: **!**

I am cold**.** What is the temperature**?** It is freezing**!**

Read each sentence. Write the correct end mark.

1. We had pizza for lunch _____

2. I love pizza _____

3. Salad goes with pizza _____

4. Pizza is so messy _____

5. Do you like pizza _____

Rewrite each sentence with the correct end mark.

6. Dad grilled fish for dinner

_____

7. Do you like fish

_____

End Marks

An end mark is the punctuation that comes at the end of a sentence.

Statements, or telling sentences, end in a period: **.**
Sentences that ask a question end in a question mark: **?**
Sentences that show strong feeling end in an exclamation mark: **!**

> It is time for the race**.** Who is that runner**?**
> She is so fast**!**

Read each sentence. Write the correct end mark.

1. The birthday party is next Tuesday _____ .

2. I can't wait _____

3. Will you come to my party _____

4. It is at my house _____

5. It will be lots of fun _____

Rewrite each sentence with the correct end mark.

6. Mom bought a cake

_____

7. This cake is yummy

_____

End Marks

An end mark is the punctuation that comes at the end of a sentence.

Statements, or telling sentences, end in a period: **.**
Sentences that ask a question end in a question mark: **?**
Sentences that show strong feeling end in an exclamation mark: **!**

> The lion has a fluffy mane.   Where are you?
> Don't talk!

Read each sentence. Write the correct end mark.

1. Natalie dropped the box _____

2. The phone beeped _____

3. That turtle is so slow _____

4. Can you hear me _____

5. Don't move _____

Rewrite each sentence with the correct end mark.

6. What is your favorite book

_____

7. I love that book

_____

Capitalization: Titles and Names

The names of people and their titles are proper nouns. Each main word in a name or title should begin with a capital letter.

Mr. Allan Davis is my father.

Officer Jones visited our school.

King George lived a long time ago.

Circle the person's title and name in each sentence. Then write the title and name correctly on the line.

1. mayor joan reed cut the ribbon. _____

2. My dentist is dr. ronald worth. _____

3. The new principal is ms. sharon hill. _____

4. My teacher is mr. brett burke. _____

5. The queen's son is prince charles. _____

6. I visited my neighbor, mrs. jean dwyer.

_____

7. We learned about president abraham lincoln.

_____

Capitalization: Days, Months, Holidays

The days of the week, the months of the year, and national holidays are proper nouns. Each main word in a proper noun should begin with a capital letter.

School starts on **Monday**.

My birthday is in **October**.

We eat turkey on **Thanksgiving**.

Circle the day, month, or holiday in each sentence. Then write it correctly on the line.

1. The new year begins on january 1. _____

2. My dance class is on thursday. _____

3. People dress up on halloween. _____

4. Mom and Dad have birthdays in march. _____

5. We went to a parade on independence day.

_____

6. My family went on vacation in july. _____

7. Trash pickup is on monday. _____

Capitalization

> Always capitalize the first word in a sentence.
>
> **It** was vacation.
>
> **School** was closed.

Read each sentence. Rewrite it correctly on the line.

1. we went to the beach.

_____

2. there were giant waves!

_____

3. my brother jumped in.

_____

4. a wave pushed me down!

_____

5. the water was icy cold!

_____

6. we wrapped ourselves in towels.

_____

Capitalization

Always capitalize the first word in a sentence, and the personal pronoun **I**.

    He and **I** play soccer.

    I am the goalie.

Read each sentence. Rewrite it correctly on the line.

1. i play baseball.

_____

2. Jack and i are on the same team.

_____

3. jack is a pitcher.

_____

4. i play first base.

_____

5. Jack and i practice together.

_____

6. we play catch in my yard.

_____

 Conquer Grammar • Grade 1 • © Newmark Learning, LLC

Simple Sentences

A sentence tells a complete thought. A simple sentence has a single noun, or subject, and a verb, or action word.

I see a bird.   **Subject:** I   **Verb:** see

The bird is small.   **Subject:** bird   **Verb:** is

Read each sentence. Circle which is missing, the subject or the verb.

1. Nicole the toys away.   (subject, verb)

2. Do want it?   (subject, verb)

3. The geese away.   (subject, verb)

4. am going.   (subject, verb)

5. Olivia on the swing.   (subject, verb)

6. got up.   (subject, verb)

7. Ilana brown hair.   (subject, verb)

8. We in the pool.   (subject, verb)

Simple Sentences

A sentence tells a complete thought. A simple sentence has a single noun, or subject, and a verb, or action word.

I draw.   **Subject:** I   **Verb:** draw

I pet the cat. **Subject:** I   **Verb:** pet

Read each sentence. Determine which is missing, the subject or the verb. Rewrite each sentence. Add the correct verb or subject in the parentheses ( ).

1. Our class big. (is, are)

_____

2. We the museum. (visit, travel)

_____

3. saw a painting. (have, I)

_____

4. Lunch good. (was, are)

_____

5. We the bus. (rode, have)

_____

Compound Sentences

A compound sentence is made up of two simple sentences that are joined by a comma and a conjunction, such as **and, but, or,** or **so.**

I play softball**, but** my brother plays basketball.

We went to the circus**, and** we got peanuts.

Combine each pair of simple sentences to make a compound sentence. Add a comma and the conjunction in the parentheses ( ). Write the compound sentence.

1. I want to go outside. It is raining. (but)

_____

2. We can eat now. We can eat later. (or)

_____

3. Jon got a game. Then he played it. (and)

_____

4. It stopped raining. We went outside. (so)

_____

5. I want ice cream. I have to finish dinner. (but)

_____

Compound Sentences

A compound sentence is made up of two simple sentences that are joined by a comma and a conjunction, such as **and, but, or,** or **so.**

We can eat pasta, **or** we can eat rice.

I would like to sing, **but** I have a sore throat.

Combine each pair of simple sentences to make a compound sentence. Add a comma and the conjunction in the parentheses ( ). Write the compound sentence.

1. Skunks are cute. They smell bad. (but)

_____

2. My dog has four legs. My bird has two wings. (and)

_____

3. We are tired. We will take a nap. (so)

_____

4. Tony will play piano. He will play violin. (or)

_____

5. Anna likes math. She likes science. (and)

_____

Compound Sentences

A compound sentence is made up of two simple sentences that are joined by a comma and a conjunction, such as **and, but, or,** or **so.**

We can stay home**, or** we can go to the park.

Cara wants to run**, but** she hurt her leg.

Combine each pair of simple sentences to make a compound sentence. Add a comma and the conjunction in the parentheses ( ). Write the compound sentence.

1. Carlos went to Spain. He saw many sites. (and)

_____

2. We can sing. We can dance. (or)

_____

3. The baby woke up. I got up to play with her. (so)

_____

4. Rico likes eggs for breakfast. I like pancakes. (but)

_____

5. I want to play outside. I have homework. (but)

_____

Different Kinds of Sentences

There are different kinds of sentences. The end mark reveals the sentence type.

Statement: I bought a glove**.**

Question: When is your next game**?**

Strong Feeling: Baseball is fun**!**

Determine the sentence type and rewrite each sentence with the correct end mark.

1. What time is it _____

2. I love to sing _____

3. I read my book _____

4. Do you like to dance _____

5. You ran so fast _____

6. My birthday is today _____

7. Where is the cat _____

8. Let's go _____

 Conquer Grammar • Grade 1 • © Newmark Learning, LLC

Expand Imperative Sentences

An imperative sentence gives a command. You can expand imperative sentences by adding details that answer **when**, **where**, **what**, **why**, or **how**.

Sit down **quietly**.

Choose the correct detail from the box to expand each imperative sentence. Write it on the line.

out to play	at the table	before dinner	to your brother	to the library

1. Return the book _____.

2. Take the dog _____.

3. Clean your room _____.

4. Do your homework _____.

5. Be nice _____.

Expand Imperative and Exclamatory Sentences

An imperative sentence gives a command. An exclamatory sentence shows excitement. You can expand imperative and exclamatory sentences by adding details that answer **when**, **where**, **what**, **why**, or **how**.

Imperative:
Go to your room **right now.**

Exclamatory:
I can't wait **to go to the beach!**

Choose the correct detail from the box to expand each sentence. Write it on the line, with the correct end mark.

for pie	to pick apples	sour and green	to my teacher	with ice cream

1. We are going to the orchard _____

2. I hate apples that are _____

3. Mom uses these apples _____

4. I love pie _____

5. I will take an apple _____

Expand Imperative and Exclamatory Sentences

An imperative sentence gives a command. An exclamatory sentence shows excitement. You can expand imperative and exclamatory sentences by adding details that answer **when**, **where**, **what**, **why**, or **how**.

Imperative:
Listen **to the directions.**

Exclamatory:
The **monster** costume was scary**!**

Add details to expand each imperative or exclamatory sentence by adding details.

1. The dog barked _____!

2. There is a bird _____.

3. Write a response _____.

4. I really want to go _____!

5. Read the directions before you begin _____.

Name _____ Date _____

Expand Declarative and Exclamatory Sentences

Declarative sentences make statements. Exclamatory sentences show excitement. You can expand declarative and exclamatory sentences by adding details that answer **when**, **where**, **what**, **why**, or **how**.

Declarative:	**Exclamatory:**
We took a bus **across town** to the game**.**	I scored a goal **at today's game!**

From the box, choose the correct detail to expand each sentence. Write it on the line with the correct end mark.

homemade and yummy	lots of fun games	this afternoon	named Sunny	at the fair

1. We went to the fair _____

2. We played _____

3. I won a goldfish _____

4. There was food that was _____

5. I had a blast _____

     Conquer Grammar • Grade 1 • © Newmark Learning, LLC

Expand Declarative
and Interrogative Sentences

Declarative sentences make statements. Interrogative sentences ask questions. You can expand declarative and interrogative sentences by adding details that answer **when**, **where**, **what**, **why**, or **how**.

Declarative:
We plant vegetables **at the market.**

Interrogative:
Would you like to go **home?**

Add details to expand each declarative or interrogative sentence.

1. We can watch the video _____.

2. Who made that _____?

3. We learn _____.

4. Will you come _____?

5. We visited her _____.

6. Where do you want to go _____?

Name _____ Date _____

Expand Declarative and Imperative Sentences

Declarative sentences make statements. Imperative sentences give commands. You can expand declarative and imperative sentences by adding details that answer **when**, **where**, **what**, **why**, or **how**.

Declarative:
We can visit Grandpa so **he isn't lonely.**

Imperative:
Look in your room **for your book.**

From the box, choose a detail to expand each declarative or imperative sentence. Write it on the line.

at the door	and come downstairs	of eggs and toast	at school	for school

1. It's time to wake up _____

2. Get dressed _____

3. Your breakfast _____ is ready.

4. There is your backpack _____

5. Have a great day _____

Expand Declarative and Imperative Sentences

Declarative sentences make statements. Imperative sentences give commands. You can expand declarative and imperative sentences by adding details that answer **when**, **where**, **what**, **why**, or **how**.

Declarative:
We can write letters **to show that we care.**

Imperative:
Get enough sleep and play outside **to stay healthy.**

Add details to expand each declarative or imperative sentence.

1. Blow out the candles _____.

2. I want to try _____.

3. Tom cooks _____.

4. Walk the dog _____.

5. Hand me the toy _____.

Name _____ Date _____

Expand Compound Declarative Sentences

Compound declarative sentences include two complete statements. You can expand declarative sentences by adding details that answer **when**, **where**, **what**, **why**, or **how**.

The test was hard, but I did well **because I studied.**

It started to rain **during our game**, so we went inside.

Add details to expand each compound declarative sentence.

1. I lost, and I felt sad.

_____

2. The baby cried because he was hungry.

_____

3. Suzie jumped, but I couldn't.

_____

4. The teacher smiled, so I smiled back.

_____

Conquer Grammar • Grade 1 • © Newmark Learning, LLC

Expand Compound Interrogative Sentences

Compound interrogative sentences include two complete questions. You can expand interrogative sentences by adding details that answer **when**, **where**, **what**, **why**, or **how**.

> Did you lose a **red, striped** hat, and is this yours**?**
>
> Do you want to play **soccer with us**, or do you want to watch**?**

Add details to expand each compound interrogative sentence.

1. Should we go, or should we stay?

_____

2. Is Jade moving, or is she staying?

_____

3. Is Rebecca here, or is she home?

_____

4. Is that the last, or are there more?

_____

Answer Key

Page 8

Name _____ Date _____

Common and Proper Nouns

A common noun names any person, place, or thing.
A proper noun names a specific person, place, or thing.
Each main word in a proper noun should begin with a
capital letter.

Common Noun	Proper Noun
friend	Sophie
ocean	Pacific
day	Monday

Read each sentence. Write the proper noun on the line.

1. Mrs. Ortiz lived near an empty lot. _Mrs. Ortiz_

2. Last Saturday, she planted a garden. _Saturday_

3. Her friends on Main Street helped. _Main Street_

4. Sophie weeded. _Sophie_

5. Julian planted seeds. _Julian_

6. By April, flowers had sprouted. _April_

7. By May, all the flowers had bloomed. _May_

8. Juan likes to play in the garden. _Juan_

8   Conquer Grammar • Grade 1 • © Newmark Learning, LLC

Page 9

Name _____ Date _____

Common and Proper Nouns

A common noun names any person, place, or thing.
A proper noun names specific person, place, or thing.
Each main word in a proper noun should begin with a
capital letter.

Common Noun	Proper Noun
girl	Lucy
city	Dallas
country	United States

Draw a line under the proper noun in each sentence.

1. My favorite team is the Red Sox.

2. They play in Boston.

3. They won the World Series Championships eight times!

**Choose a proper noun from the box to complete
each sentence. Write it on the line.**

San Diego Zoo   California   Vanessa

4. _Vanessa_ and I love zoos!

5. There are lots of zoos in _California_.

6. We will visit the _San Diego Zoo_ next.

Conquer Grammar • Grade 1 • © Newmark Learning, LLC   9

Page 10

Name _____ Date _____

Common and Proper Nouns

A common noun names any person, place, or thing.
A proper noun names a specific person, place, or thing.
Each main word in a proper noun should begin with a
capital letter.

Common Noun: The **girl** has a kitten.

Proper Noun: **Kate** has a kitten.

**Circle the proper noun in each sentence. Write it
correctly on the line.**

1. (samantha) hopes to win the game. _Samantha_

2. He visited (new york). _New York_

3. There is a concert this (saturday). _Saturday_

4. My friend (maria) is funny. _Maria_

5. The family moved here from (arizona). _Arizona_

6. The team meets every (friday). _Friday_

7. My aunt lives in (california). _California_

8. I like the cold weather in (alaska). _Alaska_

10   Conquer Grammar • Grade 1 • © Newmark Learning, LLC

Page 11

Name _____ Date _____

Common and Proper Nouns

A common noun names any person, place, or thing.
A proper noun names specific person, place, or thing.
Each main word in a proper noun should begin with a
capital letter.

People	Places	Things
Anna	Cleveland	Lake Erie
Nana	Africa	White House

**Underline the proper noun in each sentence.
Then write it correctly on the line.**

1. I live in brooklyn. _Brooklyn_

2. I have a twin brother, nate. _Nate_

3. We play in prospect park. _Prospect Park_

4. We walk over the brooklyn bridge. _Brooklyn Bridge_

Rewrite each sentence with correct capitalization.

5. We like to eat in chinatown.
   We like to eat in Chinatown.

6. Our favorite restaurant is red lotus.
   Our favorite restaurant is Red Lotus.

Conquer Grammar • Grade 1 • © Newmark Learning, LLC   11

Answer Key

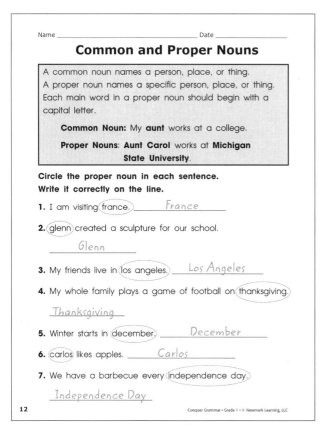

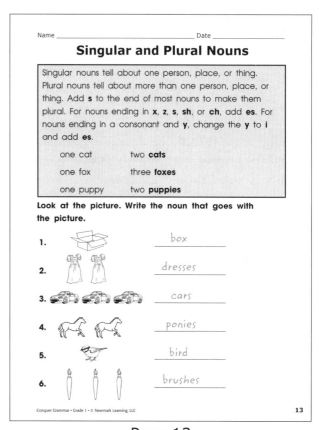

Page 12

Page 13

Page 14

Page 15

Answer Key

Page 16

Possessive Nouns

Possessive nouns show that a person, place, or thing has or owns something. Add an apostrophe ' and an s to turn most singular nouns into possessive nouns.

The park of the town is big.

The town's park is big.

Write the possessive phrase for the underlined words.

1. The wing of the bird is red. _bird's wing_

2. The skin of the baby is soft. _baby's skin_

3. Where is the key of Paul? _Paul's key_

4. We washed the car of Dad. _Dad's car_

5. The bowl of the dog is broken. _dog's bowl_

6. The hat of Kate is lost. _Kate's hat_

7. The window of the car is open. _car's window_

8. Please walk the dog of the neighbor. _neighbor's dog_

Page 17

Singular and Plural Verbs

Add **s** to the end of most verbs to make them singular. For verbs ending in **x**, **z**, **s**, **sh**, or **ch**, add **es**. For verbs ending in a consonant and **y**, change the **y** to **i** and add **es**. Do not add **s** to the end of a plural verb.

Singular Verb	Plural Verb
The tiger **roars**.	The tigers **roar**.
The girl **fixes** the bike.	The girls **fix** the bike.
The hamster **scurries**.	The hamsters **scurry**.

Read each sentence. Underline the correct verb.

1. Jorge and Dad (drive, drives) to the lake.

2. The sun (shine, shines) in the sky.

3. Jorge (try, tries).

4. Dad (help, helps) him.

5. Jorge (learn, learns) fast.

Choose the correct verb. Write it on the line.

6. They _watch_. (watch, watches)

7. Jorge _wishes_ on a star. (wish, wishes)

Page 18

Singular and Plural Verbs

Singular verbs tell about the action of one person, place, or thing. Plural verbs tell about the action of more than one person, place, or thing. Add **s** to the end of most verbs to make them singular. A plural verb should not end in **s**.

One cat **sleeps**.

Two cats **sleep**.

Choose the correct verb. Write it on the line.

1. The bees _look_ for honey. (look, looks)

2. The bird _finds_ berries. (find, finds)

3. The rabbit _eats_ grass. (eat, eats)

4. The squirrels _hunt_ for nuts. (hunt, hunts)

5. The foxes _hide_ their food. (hide, hides)

6. The sun _sets_. (set, sets)

7. The animals _sleep_. (sleep, sleeps)

8. The stars _shine_. (shine, shines)

Page 19

Present Tense Verbs

Verbs are action words. Present tense verbs tell about actions that are happening right now. For the present tense, add **-s** or **-es** if the subject of a sentence is singular. Do not add **-s** or **-es** if the subject is plural.

Fred **likes** the color yellow.

Cara and Raul **like** the movie.

Write the present tense form of the verb in the parentheses ( ).

1. Davis (play) soccer. _plays_

2. Marta and Pat (answer) questions. _answer_

3. Dad (call) to us. _calls_

4. The players (run) around the field. _run_

5. Connor (eat) the sandwich. _eats_

6. Grandma (drive) us. _drives_

Answer Key

Name _____ Date _____

Present Tense Verbs

Verbs are action words. Present tense verbs tell about actions that are happening right now. For the present tense, add **-s** or **-es** if the subject of a sentence is singular. Do not add **-s** or **-es** if the subject is plural.

Sam **plays** soccer on Saturdays.

Billy and Mia **play** tag.

Write the present tense form of the verb in the parentheses ( ).

1. Lisa, José, and Vinny (build) a fort. _build_

2. They (use) branches. _use_

3. Vinny (ask) Mom for a sheet. _asks_

4. Mom (give) him a sheet. _gives_

5. They (finish) the fort. _finish_

6. Mom (bring) them a snack. _brings_

20

Conquer Grammar • Grade 1 • © Newmark Learning, LLC

Page 20

Name _____ Date _____

Present Tense Verbs

Verbs are action words. Present tense verbs tell about actions that are happening right now. For the present tense, add **-s** or **-es** if the subject of a sentence is singular. Do not add **-s** or **-es** if the subject is plural.

Rose **runs** around the house.

Lisa and Austin **run** around the tree.

Write the present tense form of the verb in the parentheses ( ).

1. Ed and Robbie (play) catch. _play_

2. The dog (watch) them. _watches_

3. Ed (toss) the ball. _tosses_

4. Robbie (miss) the ball. _misses_

5. The dog (catch) it! _catches_

6. Ed and Robbie (laugh). _laugh_

Conquer Grammar • Grade 1 • © Newmark Learning, LLC

21

Page 21

Name _____ Date _____

Past Tense Verbs

Past tense verbs tell about actions that already happened. Past tense verbs often end in **-ed**.

He **looked** both ways.

He **crossed** the street.

Write the past tense form of the verb in the parentheses ( ).

1. We (look) at the sky. _looked_

2. We (learn) about stars. _learned_

3. I (help) Matt see. _helped_

4. The sun (warm) Sara's face. _warmed_

5. The clouds (block) the sun. _blocked_

6. It (start) to rain. _started_

7. I (listen) to music for an hour. _listened_

22

Conquer Grammar • Grade 1 • © Newmark Learning, LLC

Page 22

Name _____ Date _____

Past Tense Verbs

Past tense verbs tell about actions that already happened. Past tense verbs often end in **-ed**.

We **jumped** high.

We **reached** for the stars.

Write the past tense form of the verb.

1. We _walked_ home from school.
walk

2. Liam and I _played_ in the yard.
play

3. We _climbed_ the tree.
climb

4. Mom _called_ us inside.
call

5. We all _helped_ Mom cook dinner.
help

6. Mom _asked_ me to set the table.
ask

Conquer Grammar • Grade 1 • © Newmark Learning, LLC

23

Page 23

Answer Key

Page 24

Conquer Grammar • Grade 1 • © Newmark Learning, LLC

Name _____ Date _____

Irregular Past Tense Verbs

Past tense verbs tell about actions that already happened. Past tense verbs that do not end in **-ed** are irregular. Some examples of verbs and their irregular past tense forms include **break/broke, wear/wore, know/knew, teach/taught.**

Pablo **broke** the glass.

Kim **wore** a red cap.

Tom **drew** a picture.

Underline the verb in each sentence. Then write the past tense form of the verb.

1. I know the answer. _____knew_____

2. School begin last month. _____began_____

3. Amy know where to look for the cat. _____knew_____

4. Richard break the vase. _____broke_____

5. Rita wear her new shoes. _____wore_____

6. She teach the class. _____taught_____

24

Page 25

Name _____ Date _____

Future Tense Verbs

Future tense verbs tell about actions that will happen at a later time. To form the future tense, place the word **will** in front of the verb.

Birds **will build** nests in the spring.

Mom **will plant** tomatoes in June.

Write the future tense form of the verb in the parentheses ( ).

1. I (make) the team. _____will make_____

2. I (practice) every day. _____will practice_____

3. Dad (teach) me to hit. _____will teach_____

4. We (toss) the ball. _____will toss_____

5. Mom (run) with me. _____will run_____

6. I (play) baseball. _____will play_____

Conquer Grammar • Grade 1 • © Newmark Learning, LLC

25

Page 26

Name _____ Date _____

Future Tense Verbs

Future tense verbs tell about actions that will happen at a later time. To form the future tense, place the word **will** in front of the verb.

Tomorrow, we **will go** to the library.

I **will do** my homework after school.

Write the future tense form of the verb in the parentheses ( ).

1. I (be) an astronaut one day. _____will be_____

2. I (wear) a space suit. _____will wear_____

3. I (fly) the space ship. _____will fly_____

4. My ship (land) on Mars. _____will land_____

5. My family (miss) me. _____will miss_____

6. We (talk) using computers. _____will talk_____

26

Conquer Grammar • Grade 1 • © Newmark Learning, LLC

Page 27

Name _____ Date _____

Verb Tenses

The tense of a verb shows when the action happens. To form the past tense of most verbs, add **-ed**. For the present tense, either use the verb as is or add **-s** or **-es**. To form the future tense, place the word **will** in front of the verb.

Past:
Last month, Jonah **played** golf.

Present:
Today, Jonah **plays** hockey.

Future:
Next week, Jonah **will play** soccer.

Read each sentence. Write present, past, or future for the underlined verb.

1. Last year, we moved here. _____past_____

2. I started a new school. _____past_____

3. We adopted a dog. _____past_____

4. I walk the dog to the park. _____present_____

5. I will play with the dog after school every day.

_____future_____

Choose the correct verb. Write it on the line.

6. Last week, I _____called_____ my cousins. (called, will call)

7. Next week, we _____will visit_____ them. (visited, will visit)

Conquer Grammar • Grade 1 • © Newmark Learning, LLC

27

Conquer Grammar • Grade 1 • © Newmark Learning, LLC

Answer Key

Conquer Grammar • Grade 1 • © Newmark Learning, LLC

Page 28

Name _____ Date _____

Verb Tenses

The tense of a verb shows when the action happens. To form the past tense of most verbs, add **-ed**. For the present tense, either use the verb as is or add **-s** or **-es**. To form the future tense, place the word **will** in front of the verb.

Past:
Last week, Alex **cleaned** the hamster cage.

Present:
This week, I **clean** the hamster cage.

Future:
Next week, Jane **will clean** the hamster cage.

Read each sentence. Write *present*, *past*, or *future* for the underlined verb.

1. Yesterday, I walked home from school. _____ *past*

2. I talked with my best friends. _____ *past*

3. I will walk home if the sun is out. _____ *future*

4. Dad will drive me on rainy days. _____ *future*

5. I like to walk. _____ *present*

Complete each sentence with one of the following verbs: *played, will play, play.*

6. Next month, we *will play* soccer.

7. Last month, we *played* basketball.

28

Conquer Grammar • Grade 1 • © Newmark Learning, LLC

Page 29

Name _____ Date _____

Verb Tenses

The tense of a verb shows when the action happens. To form the past tense of most verbs, add **-ed**. For the present tense, either use the verb as is or add **-s** or **-es**. To form the future tense, place the word **will** in front of the verb.

Past:
Yesterday, we **visited** a museum.

Present:
Now, we **visit** a zoo.

Future:
Tomorrow, we **will visit** a water park.

Read each sentence. Write *present*, *past*, or *future* for the underlined verb.

1. Last year, we painted my room. _____ *past*

2. Next spring, I will play baseball. _____ *future*

3. Ella kicks the ball. _____ *present*

4. We discovered a raccoon. _____ *past*

5. Mr. Jones will speak on Monday. _____ *future*

Choose the correct verb. Write it on the line.

6. Last winter, we *traveled* to Florida. (travel, traveled)

7. Suzy *walks* the dog now. (walked, walks)

Conquer Grammar • Grade 1 • © Newmark Learning, LLC

29

Page 30

Name _____ Date _____

Verb Tenses

The tense of a verb shows when the action happens. To form the past tense of most verbs, add **-ed**. For the present tense, either use the verb as is or add **-s** or **-es**. To form the future tense, place the word **will** in front of the verb.

Past:
Last year, Jenna **danced** ballet.

Present:
This year, Jenna **dances** jazz.

Future:
Next year, Jenna **will dance** hip-hop.

Choose the correct verb. Write it on the line.

1. Tomorrow, we *will bake* muffins. (baked, will bake)

2. Last week, we *learned* about trees. (learn, learned)

3. Arlo *tosses* the ball now. (tossed, tosses)

4. This morning, Mr. Bensz *cooked* eggs. (cook, cooked)

5. The leaves *will change* color in the fall. (will change, changed)

Read each sentence. Write *present*, *past*, or *future* for the underlined verb.

6. After practice, Jordan rubbed her legs. _____ *past*

7. I like animals. _____ *present*

30

Conquer Grammar • Grade 1 • © Newmark Learning, LLC

Page 31

Name _____ Date _____

Singular Nouns with Matching Verbs

A singular noun names one person, place, or thing. In a sentence, the noun or subject and the verb must match. A singular noun takes a singular verb. Singular verbs end in **-s** or **-es**.

The <u>girl</u> **cooks** rice.
The <u>boy</u> **bakes** a cake.

Write the singular form of the verb to match the singular noun.

1. Justin _____ *looks* across the street.
look

2. Milu _____ *stands* next to him.
stand

3. A friend _____ *waves* to them.
wave

4. The sun _____ *starts* to set.
start

5. Mom _____ *calls* Justin and Milu.
call

6. She _____ *needs* help with dinner.
need

Conquer Grammar • Grade 1 • © Newmark Learning, LLC

31

Answer Key

Plural Nouns with Matching Verbs

A plural noun names more than one person, place, or thing. In a sentence, the noun or subject and the verb must match. A plural noun takes a plural verb. Plural verbs do not end in **-s**.

The <u>kids</u> **walk** down the street.

<u>Tim and Mia</u> **run** around the track.

Read each sentence. Underline the correct verb.

1. The dogs (<u>chase</u>, chases) the cats.

2. The boys (<u>wash</u>, washes) the car.

3. The teachers (reads, <u>read</u>) the directions.

4. The students (writes, <u>write</u>) their names.

5. The swans (<u>glide</u>, glides) across the pond.

Choose the correct verb. Write it on the line.

6. The babies ____nap____. (nap, naps)

7. The toddlers ____play____. (plays, play)

8. The girls ____skip____. (skip, skips)

Conquer Grammar • Grade 1 • © Newmark Learning, LLC

Page 32

Singular and Plural Nouns with Matching Verbs

In a sentence, the noun or subject and the verb must match. A singular noun takes a singular verb. A plural noun takes a plural verb.

One <u>girl</u> **throws** a ball.

Two <u>girls</u> **throw** a ball.

Choose the correct verb. Write it on the line.

1. The birds ____sing____ in the tree. (sing, sings)

2. The ants ____crawl____ in the dirt. (crawl, crawls)

3. A fly ____buzzes____ in my ear. (buzz, buzzes)

4. A butterfly ____lands____ on my hand. (land, lands)

5. A snake ____slides____ through the grass. (slide, slides)

Read each sentence. Underline the correct verb.

6. The spider (spin, <u>spins</u>) a web.

7. The dog (<u>bark</u>, barks) at a squirrel.

8. The squirrels (<u>eat</u>, eats) acorns.

Conquer Grammar • Grade 1 • © Newmark Learning, LLC

Page 33

Singular and Plural Nouns with Matching Verbs

In a sentence, the noun or subject and the verb must match. A singular noun takes a singular verb. A plural noun takes a plural verb.

Singular: The <u>flower</u> **grows**.

Plural: The <u>flowers</u> **grow**.

Read each sentence. Underline the correct verb.

1. The baby (sleep, <u>sleeps</u>) in her crib.

2. Dad (feed, <u>feeds</u>) the baby.

3. Mom and Dad (<u>play</u>, plays) with the baby.

4. Mom and Dad (<u>sing</u>, sings) to the baby.

5. The baby (clap, <u>claps</u>).

Choose the correct verb. Write it on the line.

6. The baby ____watches____. (watch, watches)

7. She ____starts____ to sing. (start, starts)

8. The baby ____learns____ quickly. (learn, learns)

Conquer Grammar • Grade 1 • © Newmark Learning, LLC

Page 34

Singular and Plural Nouns with Matching Verbs

In a sentence, the noun or subject and the verb must match. A singular noun takes a singular verb. A plural noun takes a plural verb.

Singular: The <u>frog</u> **jumps**.

Plural: The two <u>frogs</u> **jump**.

Read each sentence. Underline the correct verb.

1. My friends (<u>walk</u>, walks) to the garden.

2. Tina (plant, <u>plants</u>) seeds.

3. John (water, <u>waters</u>) the garden.

4. Fran and Molly (<u>pull</u>, pulls) out weeds.

5. Vegetables (<u>grow</u>, grows) in the spring.

Choose the correct verb. Write it on the line.

6. Our parents ____help____ cook the vegetables. (help, helps)

7. I ____like____ to grow my food! (like, likes)

Conquer Grammar • Grade 1 • © Newmark Learning, LLC

Page 35

Answer Key

Name _____ Date _____

Singular and Plural Nouns with Matching Verbs

In a sentence, the noun or subject and the verb must match. A singular noun takes a singular verb. A plural noun takes a plural verb.

One <u>lion</u> **roars**.

Two <u>lions</u> **roar**.

Choose the correct verb. Write it on the line.

1. The family ___visits___ New York City. (visit, visits)

2. Dina ___looks___ at the skyscrapers. (look, looks)

3. The family ___rides___ the subway. (ride, rides)

4. Lucas and Estella ___take___ pictures. (take, takes)

Read each sentence. Underline the correct verb.

5. Good students (<u>follow</u>, follows) rules.

6. Rules (<u>keep</u>, keeps) us safe.

7. The teacher (lead, <u>leads</u>) the class.

8. The principal (speak, <u>speaks</u>) at the meeting.

36   Conquer Grammar • Grade 1 • © Newmark Learning, LLC

Page 36

Name _____ Date _____

Personal Pronouns

Pronouns are words that take the place of nouns. **I**, **he**, **she**, **we**, **they**, and **them** are personal pronouns. Personal pronouns can be used to avoid repetition of the noun.

Noun	Personal Pronoun
Mary goes to camp.	**She** goes to camp.

Write the personal pronoun *he, she, they, him,* or *them* for the underlined word or words.

1. <u>Julie</u> lives in the city. ___She___

2. <u>David</u> lives in the country. ___He___

3. Julie visits <u>David</u>. ___him___

4. <u>Julie and David</u> climb trees. ___They___

5. The cat follows <u>Julie and David</u>! ___them___

6. <u>Julie</u> loves to visit David. ___She___

7. <u>Julie and David</u> have lots of fun together. ___They___

Conquer Grammar • Grade 1 • © Newmark Learning, LLC   37

Page 37

Name _____ Date _____

Personal Pronouns

Pronouns are words that take the place of nouns. **I**, **he**, **she**, **we**, **they**, and **them** are personal pronouns. Personal pronouns can be used to avoid repetition of the noun.

Noun	Personal Pronoun
James has a goldfish.	**He** has a goldfish.
Maggie and **Janel** painted the room.	**They** painted the room.

Choose the correct personal pronoun from the box to complete each sentence. Write it on the line.

He	She	I	They	It

1. I live in a house. ___It___ has a flat roof.

2. My name is Alina. ___I___ am eight years old.

3. Jorge lives across the street. ___He___ has a twin sister.

4. Martina is Jorge's sister. ___She___ and Jorge look alike.

5. I like to play with Jorge and Martina. ___They___ are my friends.

38   Conquer Grammar • Grade 1 • © Newmark Learning, LLC

Page 38

Name _____ Date _____

Possessive Pronouns

Pronouns take the place of nouns. Possessive pronouns show ownership. **My**, **his**, **her**, **our**, and **their** are possessive pronouns.

I drink **my** milk.

Mom drinks **her** water.

Choose the correct possessive pronoun from the box to complete each sentence. Write it on the line.

my	his	her	our	their

1. Nora took ___her___ jacket.

2. Noah brought ___his___ bike.

3. I packed ___my___ backpack.

4. We ate ___our___ snacks.

5. They ate ___their___ apples.

6. I liked ___my___ banana.

Conquer Grammar • Grade 1 • © Newmark Learning, LLC   39

Page 39

Answer Key

Name _____ Date _____

Personal and Possessive Pronouns

Pronouns are words that take the place of nouns. Personal pronouns refer to specific people, places, or things. Possessive pronouns show ownership.

Personal	**Possessive**
Alex and Jan read a book.	The book is **theirs**.
He reads a book.	The book is **his**.

Write the personal pronoun *he*, *she*, or *they* for the underlined word or words.

1. <u>Mia</u> gets a bowl. _She_

2. <u>Dad</u> adds lettuce. _He_

3. <u>Mia and Dad</u> make a salad. _They_

Write the possessive pronoun *their*, *her*, or *his* for the underlined word or words.

4. Mia adds <u>Mia's</u> carrots. _her_

5. Dad adds <u>Dad's</u> dressing. _his_

6. Mia and Dad eat <u>Mia and Dad's</u> salads. _their_

40   Conquer Grammar • Grade 1 • © Newmark Learning, LLC

Name _____ Date _____

Indefinite Pronouns

Pronouns are words that take the place of nouns. Indefinite pronouns don't refer to a specific person or thing.

Somebody broke the vase.

Nobody is in the room.

Read each sentence. Circle the indefinite pronoun.

1. (Everyone) went to the park.

2. (Someone) called me.

3. Did you forget (something?)

4. (Nobody) wanted to go home.

5. Did (anyone) lose a jacket?

Choose the correct indefinite pronoun. Write it on the line.

6. Did _someone_ knock? (someone, anything)

7. _Somebody_ is looking out the window. (Nothing, Somebody)

Conquer Grammar • Grade 1 • © Newmark Learning, LLC   41

Name _____ Date _____

Indefinite Pronouns

Pronouns are words that take the place of nouns. Indefinite pronouns don't refer to a specific person or thing.

Is **anybody** home?

Everyone must be out.

Read each sentence. Circle the indefinite pronoun.

1. (Somebody) lost a hat.

2. (Everyone) is smiling.

3. Do you want (anything) to eat?

4. (Someone) is missing.

5. Did (anyone) call Laurel?

Choose the correct indefinite pronoun. Write it on the line.

6. There is _nothing_ in the box. (anything, nothing)

7. _Nobody_ knows the answer. (Nobody, Nothing)

8. Did you talk to _anyone_? (anyone, something)

42   Conquer Grammar • Grade 1 • © Newmark Learning, LLC

Name _____ Date _____

Adjectives

Adjectives are words that describe nouns. Adjectives give details about people, places, and things. They tell about size, color, number, and kind.

The **three** boys jumped.

The **young** girls hopped.

Choose an adjective from the box to complete each sentence. Write it on the line.

heavy   sharp   two   blue   big   soft

1. Kari wears her _blue_ shirt.

2. Steve ate _two_ cookies.

3. That elephant is so _big_!

4. Don't touch the _sharp_ glass.

5. Is the backpack too _heavy_ to lift?

6. Sue likes her _soft_ blanket.

Conquer Grammar • Grade 1 • © Newmark Learning, LLC   43

Answer Key

Adjectives

Adjectives are words that describe nouns. Adjectives give details about people, places, and things. They tell about size, color, number, and kind.

Andy ate **ten** grapes.

Try some of the **delicious** pizza!

Choose an adjective from the box to complete each sentence. Write it on the line.

green	cold	one	fuzzy	loud

1. The _____loud_____ alarm hurts my ears.

2. Bees are _____fuzzy_____ insects.

3. Dad bought me _____one_____ sandwich.

4. Nathan has a _____green_____ hat.

5. I drank the _____cold_____ water.

44   Conquer Grammar • Grade 1 • © Newmark Learning, LLC

Page 44

Adjectives

Adjectives are words that describe nouns. Adjectives give details about people, places, and things. They tell about size, color, number, and kind.

Tina's cat has **green** eyes.

Stand under the **tall** tree.

Underline the adjective in each sentence.

1. Brendan wanted a <u>new</u> toy.

2. It was a <u>difficult</u> choice.

3. He liked the <u>red</u> car.

4. He also liked a <u>yellow</u> truck.

5. He chose the <u>faster</u> car.

6. He paid with <u>shiny</u> coins.

7. The clerk put the toy into a <u>paper</u> bag.

8. Brendan left the store with a <u>big</u> smile on his face.

Conquer Grammar • Grade 1 • © Newmark Learning, LLC   45

Page 45

Adjectives

Adjectives are words that describe nouns. Adjectives give details about people, places, and things. They tell about size, color, number, and kind.

Six roses are in the **tall** vase.

Read each sentence. Underline the adjective. Then write the noun it describes.

1. Ed likes <u>bright</u> sneakers. _____sneakers_____

2. Mr. Sanchez read a <u>scary</u> story. _____story_____

3. Janet ate a <u>sweet</u> apple. _____apple_____

4. What's in the <u>brown</u> box? _____box_____

5. Rabbits are <u>quiet</u> pets. _____pets_____

6. Ms. Burke drives a <u>fast</u> car. _____car_____

7. The dog has <u>long</u> fur. _____fur_____

46   Conquer Grammar • Grade 1 • © Newmark Learning, LLC

Page 46

Adjectives

Adjectives are words that describe nouns. Adjectives give details about people, places, and things. They tell about size, color, number, and kind.

The **big** library is in the **white** building.

Read each sentence. Underline the adjective. Then write the noun it describes.

1. Most spiders have <u>eight</u> eyes. _____eyes_____

2. The <u>tiny</u> ant ate a crumb. _____ant_____

3. The <u>orange</u> bug landed on me. _____bug_____

4. Don't touch the <u>red</u> ants. _____ants_____

5. I don't like <u>big</u> spiders. _____spiders_____

6. I see a <u>brown</u> earthworm. _____earthworm_____

7. Look at the <u>pretty</u> butterfly. _____butterfly_____

Conquer Grammar • Grade 1 • © Newmark Learning, LLC   47

Page 47

Answer Key

Page 48

Name _____ Date _____

Adverbs

Adverbs describe verbs. They give details about how, when, or where an action happens.

The actors spoke **clearly**.   They heard the story **before**.

I lost my pen **somewhere**.   We **quickly** ran to the store.

Read each sentence. Circle the verb and underline the adverb.

1. Sophia <u>happily</u> (agreed) to dance in the ballet.

2. The dancers (practiced) <u>daily</u>.

3. The dance company (presented) the ballet <u>outdoors</u>.

4. Sophia (performed) <u>beautifully</u>.

5. Her friends (threw) a party <u>afterward</u>.

Underline the adverb in each sentence. Then circle whether the adverb tells *how, when,* or *where*.

6. Flowers grow <u>everywhere</u>.   How   When   (Where)

7. Tom <u>carefully</u> picks them.   (How)   When   Where

8. <u>Soon</u>, he will put them into a vase.   How   (When)   Where

48   Conquer Grammar • Grade 1 • © Newmark Learning, LLC

Page 49

Name _____ Date _____

Prepositions

Prepositions connect two or more words in a sentence and show how they are related. Some prepositions show where something is. Others show where or when something happens.

Pat put the plate **on** the table.

We listen **during** story hour.

Read each sentence. Underline the preposition.

1. There is a giant tree <u>in</u> the park.

2. We sit <u>under</u> the tree.

3. Squirrels run <u>on</u> the branches.

4. The leaves turn red <u>during</u> fall.

5. Then they fall <u>to</u> the ground.

6. I love to run <u>through</u> the leaf piles.

7. The owl is <u>in</u> the tree.

8. I watch the owl <u>with</u> Mom.

Conquer Grammar • Grade 1 • © Newmark Learning, LLC   49

Page 50

Name _____ Date _____

Prepositions

Prepositions connect two or more words in a sentence and show how they are related. Some prepositions show where something is. Others show where or when something happens.

Look **beyond** the river.

There is a rainbow **in** the sky.

Read each sentence. Underline the preposition.

1. I live <u>in</u> this house.

2. My cousins live <u>across</u> the street.

3. We live <u>on</u> a quiet road.

4. The park is <u>around</u> the corner.

5. Our school is <u>beyond</u> the park.

6. The supermarket is <u>on</u> Main Street.

7. Look <u>at</u> that cat!

8. It is <u>on</u> the roof.

50   Conquer Grammar • Grade 1 • © Newmark Learning, LLC

Page 51

Name _____ Date _____

Prepositions

Prepositions connect two or more words in a sentence and show how they are related. Some prepositions show where something is. Others show where or when something happens.

We walk **on** the grass.

We swim **in** the lake.

Choose the correct preposition. Write it on the line.

1. My family is going hiking (on, in) Sunday. _on_

2. My friend Bella is coming (with, by) us. _with_

3. We are sleeping (in, at) cabins. _in_

4. We will tell stories (by, from) the fire. _by_

5. We will toast hot dogs (of, on) sticks. _on_

6. We will sing (under, at) the stars. _under_

7. I love being (in, from) the woods. _in_

8. I will wrap a blanket (around, at) me. _around_

Conquer Grammar • Grade 1 • © Newmark Learning, LLC   51

Conquer Grammar • Grade 1 • © Newmark Learning, LLC

Answer Key

Page 52

Name _____ Date _____

Prepositions

Prepositions connect two or more words in a sentence and show how they are related. Some prepositions show where something is. Others show where or when something happens.

I look **for** my glasses.

They are **on** the nightstand.

Choose the correct preposition. Write it on the line.

1. I walk (for, to) school. ___to___

2. I walk (at, with) my friends. ___with___

3. We walk (by, for) the park. ___by___

4. We look (for, in) bugs. ___for___

5. We see ants (at, on) the ground. ___on___

6. I look (at, near) my watch. ___at___

7. It is (after, under) eight o'clock! ___after___

8. We hurry (around, to) school. ___to___

52 · Conquer Grammar · Grade 1 · © Newmark Learning, LLC

Page 53

Name _____ Date _____

Prepositions

Prepositions connect two or more words in a sentence and show how they are related. Some prepositions show where something is. Others show where or when something happens.

The milk is **for** the cereal.

The cat purred **at** me.

Choose a preposition from the box to complete each sentence. Write it on the line.

at	for	in	on	through

1. The cup is ___on___ the table.

2. Meet me ___at___ 8:30 in the morning.

3. The flower is ___for___ my mother.

4. My sister is ___in___ middle school.

5. Manny walked ___through___ the garden.

6. I put the book ___on___ the desk.

7. Jacob arrived ___at___ the game first.

8. Lena wrote a poem ___for___ me.

Conquer Grammar · Grade 1 · © Newmark Learning, LLC · 53

Page 54

Name _____ Date _____

Prepositions

Prepositions help connect two words in a sentence and show how they are related. Some prepositions tell where something is. Others tell when something happens.

Walk **toward** the corner.

The clue is **on** the tree.

Choose the correct preposition from the box to complete each sentence. Write it on the line. You can use a preposition more than once.

toward	about	in	across	for	on

1. I look at the house ___across___ the street.

2. I think ___about___ my best friend.

3. Lucy moved ___across___ the country.

4. I look ___toward___ the sky.

5. The sun sets ___in___ the west.

6. Stars sparkle ___in___ the sky.

7. I wish ___for___ my friend back.

8. I call Lucy ___on___ the phone.

54 · Conquer Grammar · Grade 1 · © Newmark Learning, LLC

Page 55

Name _____ Date _____

Conjunctions

Conjunctions are linking words. They combine two short sentences into a longer sentence. **And, or, but, so,** and **because** are conjunctions.

I eat breakfast **and** then brush my teeth.

I get the bus **and** go to school.

Read each sentence. Underline the conjunction. Write it on the line.

1. I was tired, so I went to bed. ___so___

2. Is the glass full or empty? ___or___

3. Jan likes fall, but she doesn't like winter. ___but___

4. We went hiking and took pictures. ___and___

5. I took a bath because I was dirty. ___because___

6. You can do your homework now or later. ___or___

7. The sky turned gray, and it began to rain. ___and___

Conquer Grammar · Grade 1 · © Newmark Learning, LLC · 55

Answer Key

Conjunctions

Conjunctions are linking words. They combine two short sentences into a longer sentence. **And, or, but, so,** and **because** are conjunctions.

> I eat dinner, **and** then I wash the dishes.
> I read **or** play a game.

Read each sentence. Underline the conjunction. Write it on the line.

1. Cheetahs have spots, and they run fast. ___and___

2. Bears may look cute, but they are dangerous. ___but___

3. Elephants splash in the water because they love to swim.
   ___because___

4. Zebras have stripes, and no two zebras have the same pattern. ___and___

5. Snakes can be tiny or huge. ___or___

6. Lions nap during the day, so they can hunt for food at night. ___so___

56
Conquer Grammar • Grade 1 • © Newmark Learning, LLC

Page 56

Conjunctions

Conjunctions are linking words. They combine two short sentences into a longer sentence. **And, or, but, so,** and **because** are conjunctions.

> Lila can take art, **or** she can take music.
> I want to visit Grandpa **because** I miss him.

Read each sentence. Choose the correct conjunction. Write it on the line.

1. Joel wants to swim, ___but___ it is raining.
   (but, or)

2. Luke is tired ___because___ it is late.
   (or, because)

3. We will go to the zoo, ___and___ we will see animals.
   (and, but)

4. Alice loves to draw, ___so___ she will take art.
   (but, so)

5. We can stay in, ___or___ we can go out.
   (so, or)

57
Conquer Grammar • Grade 1 • © Newmark Learning, LLC

Page 57

Conjunctions

Conjunctions are linking words. They combine two short sentences into a longer sentence. **And, or, but, so,** and **because** are conjunctions.

> I like to ride my bike **and** visit Grandma.

Use a conjunction from the box to combine each pair of sentences. Write the new sentence on the line.

because	so	and

1. The band has a drummer. The band has a piano player.
   The band has a drummer and a piano player.

2. The band played an old song. People wanted to sing along.
   The band played an old song because people
   wanted to sing along.

3. The band stopped playing. The band could rest.
   The band stopped playing so they could rest.

4. The crowd cheered. The crowd asked for more songs.
   The crowd cheered and asked for more songs.

58
Conquer Grammar • Grade 1 • © Newmark Learning, LLC

Page 58

Conjunctions

Conjunctions are linking words. They combine two short sentences into a longer sentence. **And, or, but, so,** and **because** are conjunctions. Place a comma before the conjunction **but.**

> The bush has green leaves. The bush has purple flowers.
> The bush has green leaves, but purple flowers.

Combine each pair of sentences using the conjunction in the parentheses ( ). Write the new sentence on the line. Add a comma if necessary.

1. We were hot. We were sweaty. (and)
   We were hot and sweaty.

2. We could go to the pool. We could go to the lake. (or)
   We could go to the pool or the lake.

3. The pool is closer. We went to the pool. (so)
   The pool is closer so we went to the pool.

4. I know how to swim. I stayed near Mom. (but)
   I know how to swim, but I stayed near Mom.
   _____

59
Conquer Grammar • Grade 1 • © Newmark Learning, LLC

Page 59

Answer Key

Name _____ Date _____

Conjunctions

Conjunctions are linking words. They combine two short sentences into a longer sentence. **And, or, but, so,** and **because** are conjunctions. Place a comma before the conjunction **but.**

We can read a book **or** play outside.

Use a conjunction from the box to combine each pair of sentences. Write the compound sentence on the line.

and	but	so	or

1. Tiffany likes dogs. She does not like cats.

Tiffany likes dogs, but she does not like cats.

2. Mom gave the baby a bottle. Mom gave the baby cereal.

Mom gave the baby a bottle and cereal.

3. We will eat dinner. We will eat dessert.

We will eat dinner and dessert.

4. I can read my book. I can walk to the park.

I read my book or walk to the park.

60

Conquer Grammar • Grade 1 • © Newmark Learning, LLC

Page 60

Name _____ Date _____

Articles

The words **a**, **an**, and **the** are articles. Use **the** to tell about an exact person, place, or thing. Use **a** or **an** to tell about any person, place, or thing. Use **a** before a consonant sound and **an** before a vowel sound.

Nolan is in **the** cafeteria.

He drinks **a** carton of milk.

He eats **an** orange.

Choose the correct article. Write it on the line.

1. I'm in (an, the) city! ___the___

2. I see (a, an) skyscraper. ___a___

3. I take (a, an) taxi. ___a___

4. I ride (a, an) elevator. ___an___

5. I walk down (an, the) main street. ___the___

6. I want to get (a, an) gift for Mom. ___a___

7. I go to (an, the) store on the corner. ___the___

8. I buy her (a, an) postcard. ___a___

Conquer Grammar • Grade 1 • © Newmark Learning, LLC

61

Page 61

Name _____ Date _____

Articles

The words **a**, **an**, and **the** are articles. Use **the** to tell about an exact person, place, or thing. Use **a** or **an** to tell about any person, place, or thing. Use **a** before a consonant sound and **an** before a vowel sound.

I look in **the** desk.

There is **a** notebook.

There is also **an** eraser.

Choose the correct article. Write it on the line.

1. We visit (an, the) animal farm. ___an___

2. Pigs roll in (a, the) mud. ___the___

3. A hen lays (a, an) egg. ___an___

4. Cows chew on (an, the) grass. ___the___

5. I take (a, an) picture. ___a___

6. Chickens hop along (a, the) fence. ___the___

7. Sheep jump on (a, the) grass. ___the___

8. We learn how to milk (a, an) cow. ___a___

62

Conquer Grammar • Grade 1 • © Newmark Learning, LLC

Page 62

Name _____ Date _____

Demonstratives

This, that, these, and **those** are demonstratives. Demonstratives tell about specific people, places, or things. Use **this** and **that** with singular nouns, and **these** and **those** with plural nouns.

This is my street. **That** house is mine.

These clothes go into my closet. **Those** clothes go into my dresser.

Read each sentence. Choose the correct demonstrative. Write it on the line.

1. (These, This) zoo is huge. ___This___

2. (That, Those) giraffe is tall. ___That___

3. (This, These) monkeys are loud. ___These___

4. (These, That) lion is sleeping. ___That___

5. (Those, That) group is having a picnic. ___That___

6. (That, Those) kids are playing tag. ___Those___

7. I like to sit on (these, that) big rock. ___that___

8. Tigers climb (those, that) trees. ___those___

Conquer Grammar • Grade 1 • © Newmark Learning, LLC

63

Page 63

Answer Key

Page 64

Name _____ Date _____

Articles and Demonstratives

The words **a**, **an**, and **the** are articles. **This**, **that**, **these**, and **those** are demonstratives. Use articles and demonstratives before nouns.

    The soccer player kicked **the** ball.

    She kicked **that** ball hard!

    She got **a** goal.

Choose the correct article or demonstrative.
Write it on the line.

1. The dog chased (these, the) cat. ___the___

2. (These, Those) birds over there are pretty. ___Those___

3. I will wear (this, these) pants today. ___these___

4. Use (this, these) marker to color your picture. ___this___

5. (A, That) girl is wearing green socks. ___That___

6. Please put (a, this) juice into the cabinet. ___this___

7. Lila broke (a, an) plate. ___a___

8. Tom brought his dog to (the, these) vet. ___the___

64   Conquer Grammar • Grade 1 • © Newmark Learning, LLC

Page 65

Name _____ Date _____

Commas in Series

Use a comma to separate three or more words in a series.
    Tina likes baseball, soccer, and tennis.

Read each sentence. Write commas where needed.

1. Monkeys, tigers, and elephants live in the jungle.

2. The kitten has brown, black, and tan spots.

3. We can play tag, hopscotch, or hide-and-seek.

Rewrite each sentence using the correct punctuation.

4. Andy has blue pink and yellow markers.

    Andy has blue, pink, and yellow markers.

5. Jimmy can sing dance and juggle.

    Jimmy can sing, dance, and juggle.

6. Sam packed yogurt fruit and toast for lunch.

    Sam packed yogurt, fruit, and toast for lunch.

Conquer Grammar • Grade 1 • © Newmark Learning, LLC   65

Page 66

Name _____ Date _____

Commas in Dates and Series

Use commas in dates and to separate three or more words in a series.
    My birthday is Thursday, August 8, 2013.
    Cows, pigs, and turkeys live on the farm.

Read each sentence. Write commas where needed.

1. Birds eat seeds, fruit, and insects.

2. My brother was born on Monday, August 22, 2011.

3. You can play with Janine, Lisa, and Matt.

Rewrite each sentence using correct punctuation.

4. Nana was born on Tuesday May 15 1956.

    Nana was born on Tuesday, May 15, 1956.

5. Kim Lulu and Maddie live upstairs.

    Kim, Lulu, and Maddie live upstairs.

6. Ava went to the mall the park and the store.

    Ava went to the mall, the park, and the store.

66   Conquer Grammar • Grade 1 • © Newmark Learning, LLC

Page 67

Name _____ Date _____

Commas in Dates and Series

Use commas in dates and to separate three or more words in a series.
    We moved on Friday, July 11, 2014.
    My scarf has blue, red, and yellow stripes.

Read each sentence. Write commas where needed.

1. The new restaurant opened on Saturday, April 2, 2016.

2. The restaurant sells hamburgers, milkshakes, and fries.

3. It is open on Fridays, Saturdays, and Sundays.

Rewrite each sentence, using correct punctuation.

4. The tag sale is on Saturday June 3 2017.

    The tag sale is on Saturday, June 3, 2017.

5. Jen Tim and Lee leave for camp the next day.

    Jen, Tim, and Lee leave for camp the next day.

6. They come home on Tuesday August 22 2017.

    They come home on Tuesday, August 22, 2017.

Conquer Grammar • Grade 1 • © Newmark Learning, LLC   67

Answer Key

End Marks

An end mark is the punctuation that comes at the end of a sentence.

Statements, or telling sentences, end in a period: .
Sentences that ask a question end in a question mark: ?
Sentences that show strong feeling end in an exclamation mark: !

   Nina is eight years old.   Where are you moving?
   Hurry up!

Read each sentence. Write the correct end mark.

1. What is your phone number _?_____

2. A car has four wheels _._____

3. Watch out _!_____

4. We tiptoed down the street _._____

5. Who is with your teacher _?_____

6. Where are you going _?_____

7. I can't wait _!_____

8. Are you ready to go _?_____

68

Conquer Grammar • Grade 1 • © Newmark Learning, LLC

Page 68

End Marks

An end mark is the punctuation that comes at the end of a sentence.

Statements, or telling sentences, end in a period: .
Sentences that ask a question end in a question mark: ?
Sentences that show strong feeling end in an exclamation mark: !

   I am tired. What time is it? It is late!

Read each sentence. Write the correct end mark.

1. My name is Charlie _._____

2. What is your name _?_____

3. I live on Broom Street _._____

4. Where do you live _?_____

5. I can't believe we are neighbors _!_____

Rewrite each sentence with the correct end mark.

6. I can't wait to bake

   _I can't wait to bake!_____

7. What should we make

   _What should we make?_____

Conquer Grammar • Grade 1 • © Newmark Learning, LLC

69

Page 69

End Marks

An end mark is the punctuation that comes at the end of a sentence.

Statements, or telling sentences, end in a period: .
Sentences that ask a question end in a question mark: ?
Sentences that show strong feeling end in an exclamation mark: !

   I am cold. What is the temperature? It is freezing!

Read each sentence. Write the correct end mark.

1. We had pizza for lunch _._____

2. I love pizza _!_____

3. Salad goes with pizza _._____

4. Pizza is so messy _!_____

5. Do you like pizza _?_____

Rewrite each sentence with the correct end mark.

6. Dad grilled fish for dinner

   _Dad grilled fish for dinner._____

7. Do you like fish

   _Do you like fish?_____

70

Conquer Grammar • Grade 1 • © Newmark Learning, LLC

Page 70

End Marks

An end mark is the punctuation that comes at the end of a sentence.

Statements, or telling sentences, end in a period: .
Sentences that ask a question end in a question mark: ?
Sentences that show strong feeling end in an exclamation mark: !

   It is time for the race. Who is that runner?
   She is so fast!

Read each sentence. Write the correct end mark.

1. The birthday party is next Tuesday _._____ .

2. I can't wait _!_____

3. Will you come to my party _?_____

4. It is at my house _._____

5. It will be lots of fun _!_____

Rewrite each sentence with the correct end mark.

6. Mom bought a cake

   _Mom bought a cake._____

7. This cake is yummy

   _This cake is yummy!_____

Conquer Grammar • Grade 1 • © Newmark Learning, LLC

71

Page 71

Answer Key

Name _____ Date _____

End Marks

An end mark is the punctuation that comes at the end of a sentence.

Statements, or telling sentences, end in a period: .
Sentences that ask a question end in a question mark: ?
Sentences that show strong feeling end in an exclamation mark: !

The lion has a fluffy mane.   Where are you?
Don't talk!

Read each sentence. Write the correct end mark.

1. Natalie dropped the box .
2. The phone beeped .
3. That turtle is so slow !
4. Can you hear me ?
5. Don't move !

Rewrite each sentence with the correct end mark.

6. What is your favorite book

   What is your favorite book?

7. I love that book

   I love that book!

72   Conquer Grammar • Grade 1 • © Newmark Learning, LLC

Page 72

Name _____ Date _____

Capitalization: Titles and Names

The names of people and their titles are proper nouns. Each main word in a name or title should begin with a capital letter.

Mr. Allan Davis is my father.

Officer Jones visited our school.

King George lived a long time ago.

Circle the person's title and name in each sentence. Then write the title and name correctly on the line.

1. mayor joan reed cut the ribbon.   *Mayor Joan Reed*
2. My dentist is dr. ronald worth.   *Dr. Ronald Worth*
3. The new principal is ms. sharon hill.   *Ms. Sharon Hill*
4. My teacher is mr. brett burke.   *Mr. Brett Burke*
5. The queen's son is prince charles.   *Prince Charles*
6. I visited my neighbor, mrs. jean dwyer.

   Mrs. Jean Dwyer

7. We learned about president abraham lincoln.

   President Abraham Lincoln

Conquer Grammar • Grade 1 • © Newmark Learning, LLC   73

Page 73

Name _____ Date _____

Capitalization: Days, Months, Holidays

The days of the week, the months of the year, and national holidays are proper nouns. Each main word in a proper noun should begin with a capital letter.

School starts on **Monday**.

My birthday is in **October**.

We eat turkey on **Thanksgiving**.

Circle the day, month, or holiday in each sentence. Then write it correctly on the line.

1. The new year begins on january 1.   *January*
2. My dance class is on thursday.   *Thursday*
3. People dress up on halloween.   *Halloween*
4. Mom and Dad have birthdays in march.   *March*
5. We went to a parade on independence day.

   Independence Day

6. My family went on vacation in july.   *July*
7. Trash pickup is on monday.   *Monday*

74   Conquer Grammar • Grade 1 • © Newmark Learning, LLC

Page 74

Name _____ Date _____

Capitalization

Always capitalize the first word in a sentence.

It was vacation.

School was closed.

Read each sentence. Rewrite it correctly on the line.

1. we went to the beach.

   We went to the beach.

2. there were giant waves!

   There were giant waves!

3. my brother jumped in.

   My brother jumped in.

4. a wave pushed me down!

   A wave pushed me down!

5. the water was icy cold!

   The water was icy cold!

6. we wrapped ourselves in towels.

   We wrapped ourselves in towels.

Conquer Grammar • Grade 1 • © Newmark Learning, LLC   75

Page 75

Answer Key

Name _____ Date _____

Capitalization

Always capitalize the first word in a sentence, and the personal pronoun **I**.

He and **I** play soccer.

I am the goalie.

Read each sentence. Rewrite it correctly on the line.

1. i play baseball.

   I play baseball.

2. Jack and i are on the same team.

   Jack and I are on the same team.

3. jack is a pitcher.

   Jack is a pitcher.

4. i play first base.

   I play first base.

5. Jack and i practice together.

   Jack and I practice together.

6. we play catch in my yard.

   We play catch in my yard.

76   Conquer Grammar • Grade 1 • © Newmark Learning, LLC

Page 76

Name _____ Date _____

Simple Sentences

A sentence tells a complete thought. A simple sentence has a single noun, or subject, and a verb, or action word.

I see a bird.   **Subject:** I **Verb:** see

The bird is small. **Subject:** bird **Verb:** is

Read each sentence. Circle which is missing, the subject or the verb.

1. Nicole the toys away. (subject, (verb))

2. Do want it? ((subject), verb)

3. The geese away. (subject, (verb))

4. am going. ((subject), verb)

5. Olivia on the swing. (subject, (verb))

6. got up. ((subject), verb)

7. Ilana brown hair. (subject, (verb))

8. We in the pool. (subject, (verb))

Conquer Grammar • Grade 1 • © Newmark Learning, LLC   77

Page 77

Name _____ Date _____

Simple Sentences

A sentence tells a complete thought. A simple sentence has a single noun, or subject, and a verb, or action word.

I draw.   **Subject:** I **Verb:** draw

I pet the cat. **Subject:** I **Verb:** pet

Read each sentence. Determine which is missing, the subject or the verb. Rewrite each sentence. Add the correct verb or subject in the parentheses ( ).

1. Our class big. (is, are)

   Our class is big.

2. We the museum. (visit, travel)

   We visit the museum.

3. saw a painting. (have, I)

   I saw a painting.

4. Lunch good. (was, are)

   Lunch was good.

5. We the bus. (rode, have)

   We rode the bus.

78   Conquer Grammar • Grade 1 • © Newmark Learning, LLC

Page 78

Name _____ Date _____

Compound Sentences

A compound sentence is made up of two simple sentences that are joined by a comma and a conjunction, such as **and, but, or,** or **so.**

I play softball, **but** my brother plays basketball.

We went to the circus, **and** we got peanuts.

Combine each pair of simple sentences to make a compound sentence. Add a comma and the conjunction in the parentheses ( ). Write the compound sentence.

1. I want to go outside. It is raining. (but)

   I want to go outside, but it is raining.

2. We can eat now. We can eat later. (or)

   We can eat now, or we can eat later.

3. Jon got a game. Then he played it. (and)

   Jon got a game, and then he played it.

4. It stopped raining. We went outside. (so)

   It stopped raining, so we went outside.

5. I want ice cream. I have to finish dinner. (but)

   I want ice cream, but I have to finish dinner.

Conquer Grammar • Grade 1 • © Newmark Learning, LLC   79

Page 79

Answer Key

Name _____ Date _____

Compound Sentences

A compound sentence is made up of two simple sentences that are joined by a comma and a conjunction, such as **and, but, or,** or **so.**

We can eat pasta, **or** we can eat rice.

I would like to sing, **but** I have a sore throat.

Combine each pair of simple sentences to make a compound sentence. Add a comma and the conjunction in the parentheses ( ). Write the compound sentence.

1. Skunks are cute. They smell bad. (but)

Skunks are cute, but they smell bad.

2. My dog has four legs. My bird has two wings. (and)

My dog has four legs, and my bird has two wings.

3. We are tired. We will take a nap. (so)

We are tired, so we will take a nap.

4. Tony will play piano. He will play violin. (or)

Tony will play piano, or he will play violin.

5. Anna likes math. She likes science. (and)

Anna likes math, and she likes science.

80 · Conquer Grammar • Grade 1 • © Newmark Learning, LLC

Page 80

Name _____ Date _____

Compound Sentences

A compound sentence is made up of two simple sentences that are joined by a comma and a conjunction, such as **and, but, or,** or **so.**

We can stay home, **or** we can go to the park.

Cara wants to run, **but** she hurt her leg.

Combine each pair of simple sentences to make a compound sentence. Add a comma and the conjunction in the parentheses ( ). Write the compound sentence.

1. Carlos went to Spain. He saw many sites. (and)

Carlos went to Spain, and he saw many sites.

2. We can sing. We can dance. (or)

We can sing, or we can dance.

3. The baby woke up. I got up to play with her. (so)

The baby woke up, so I got up to play with her.

4. Rico likes eggs for breakfast. I like pancakes. (but)

Rico likes eggs for breakfast, but I like pancakes.

5. I want to play outside. I have homework. (but)

I want play outside, but I have homework.

Conquer Grammar • Grade 1 • © Newmark Learning, LLC · 81

Page 81

Name _____ Date _____

Different Kinds of Sentences

There are different kinds of sentences. The end mark reveals the sentence type.

Statement: I bought a glove.

Question: When is your next game?

Strong Feeling: Baseball is fun!

Determine the sentence type and rewrite each sentence with the correct end mark.

1. What time is it *What time is it?*

2. I love to sing *I love to sing!*

3. I read my book *I read my book.*

4. Do you like to dance *Do you like to dance?*

5. You ran so fast *You ran so fast!*

6. My birthday is today *My birthday is today.*

7. Where is the cat *Where is the cat?*

8. Let's go *Let's go!*

82 · Conquer Grammar • Grade 1 • © Newmark Learning, LLC

Page 82

Name _____ Date _____

Expand Imperative Sentences

An imperative sentence gives a command. You can expand imperative sentences by adding details that answer **when, where, what, why,** or **how.**

Sit down **quietly.**

Choose the correct detail from the box to expand each imperative sentence. Write it on the line.

out to play	at the table	before dinner	to your brother	to the library

1. Return the book *to the library* .

2. Take the dog *out to play* .

3. Clean your room *before dinner* .

4. Do your homework *at the table* .

5. Be nice *to your brother* .

Conquer Grammar • Grade 1 • © Newmark Learning, LLC · 83

Page 83

Answer Key

Name _____ Date _____

Expand Imperative
and Exclamatory Sentences

An imperative sentence gives a command. An exclamatory sentence shows excitement. You can expand imperative and exclamatory sentences by adding details that answer **when**, **where**, **what**, **why**, or **how**.

Imperative:	**Exclamatory:**
Go to your room	I can't wait **to go**
right now.	to the beach!

Choose the correct detail from the box to expand each sentence. Write it on the line, with the correct end mark.

for pie	to pick apples	sour and green	to my teacher	with ice cream

1. We are going to the orchard _to pick apples._

2. I hate apples that are _sour and green!_

3. Mom uses these apples _for pie._

4. I love pie _with ice cream!_

5. I will take an apple _to my teacher._

84   Conquer Grammar • Grade 1 • © Newmark Learning, LLC

Page 84

Name _____ Date _____

Expand Imperative
and Exclamatory Sentences

An imperative sentence gives a command. An exclamatory sentence shows excitement. You can expand imperative and exclamatory sentences by adding details that answer **when**, **where**, **what**, **why**, or **how**.

Imperative:	**Exclamatory:**
Listen **to the**	The **monster** costume
directions.	was scary!

Add details to expand each imperative or exclamatory sentence by adding details.

Sample responses are provided.

1. The dog barked _loudly_!

2. There is a bird _in the tree_.

3. Write a response _to the question_.

4. I really want to go _to the game_!

5. Read the directions before you begin _the test_.

Conquer Grammar • Grade 1 • © Newmark Learning, LLC   85

Page 85

Name _____ Date _____

Expand Declarative
and Exclamatory Sentences

Declarative sentences make statements. Exclamatory sentences show excitement. You can expand declarative and exclamatory sentences by adding details that answer **when**, **where**, **what**, **why**, or **how**.

Declarative:	**Exclamatory:**
We took a bus **across**	I scored a goal **at**
town to the game.	**today's game!**

From the box, choose the correct detail to expand each sentence. Write it on the line with the correct end mark.

homemade and yummy	lots of fun games	this afternoon	named Sunny	at the fair

1. We went to the fair _this afternoon._

2. We played _lots of fun games!_

3. I won a goldfish _named Sunny._

4. There was food that was _homemade and yummy._

5. I had a blast _at the fair!_

86   Conquer Grammar • Grade 1 • © Newmark Learning, LLC

Page 86

Name _____ Date _____

Expand Declarative
and Interrogative Sentences

Declarative sentences make statements. Interrogative sentences ask questions. You can expand declarative and interrogative sentences by adding details that answer **when**, **where**, **what**, **why**, or **how**.

Declarative:	**Interrogative:**
We plant vegetables	Would you like to go
at the market.	**home?**

Add details to expand each declarative or interrogative sentence.

Sample answers are provided.

1. We can watch the video _on my computer_.

2. Who made that _hat_?

3. We learn _in school_.

4. Will you come _to the play_?

5. We visited her _on Tuesday_.

6. Where do you want to go _tomorrow_?

Conquer Grammar • Grade 1 • © Newmark Learning, LLC   87

Page 87

Answer Key

Page 88

Name _____ Date _____

Expand Declarative and Imperative Sentences

Declarative sentences make statements. Imperative sentences give commands. You can expand declarative and imperative sentences by adding details that answer **when, where, what, why,** or **how.**

Declarative:
We can visit Grandpa so **he isn't lonely.**

Imperative:
Look in your room **for your book.**

From the box, choose a detail to expand each declarative or imperative sentence. Write it on the line.

at the door	and come downstairs	of eggs and toast	at school	for school

1. It's time to wake up _____ for school.

2. Get dressed _____ and come downstairs.

3. Your breakfast _____ of eggs and toast _____ is ready.

4. There is your backpack _____ at the door.

5. Have a great day _____ at school.

Conquer Grammar • Grade 1 • © Newmark Learning, LLC

Page 89

Name _____ Date _____

Expand Declarative and Imperative Sentences

Declarative sentences make statements. Imperative sentences give commands. You can expand declarative and imperative sentences by adding details that answer **when, where, what, why,** or **how.**

Declarative:
We can write letters **to show that we care.**

Imperative:
Get enough sleep and play outside **to stay healthy.**

Add details to expand each declarative or imperative sentence.

Sample answers are provided.

1. Blow out the candles _____ quickly.

2. I want to try _____ doing it.

3. Tom cooks _____ hamburgers.

4. Walk the dog _____ and feed him.

5. Hand me the toy _____ now.

Conquer Grammar • Grade 1 • © Newmark Learning, LLC

Page 90

Name _____ Date _____

Expand Compound Declarative Sentences

Compound declarative sentences include two complete statements. You can expand declarative sentences by adding details that answer **when, where, what, why,** or **how.**

The test was hard, but I did well **because I studied.**

It started to rain **during our game,** so we went inside**.**

Add details to expand each compound declarative sentence.

Sample answers are provided.

1. I lost, and I felt sad.

I lost the game, and I felt sad all day.

2. The baby cried because he was hungry.

The baby cried loudly because he was hungry.

3. Suzie jumped, but I couldn't.

Suzie jumped over the log, but I couldn't.

4. The teacher smiled, so I smiled back.

The teacher smiled at me, so I smiled back.

Conquer Grammar • Grade 1 • © Newmark Learning, LLC

Page 91

Name _____ Date _____

Expand Compound Interrogative Sentences

Compound interrogative sentences include two complete questions. You can expand interrogative sentences by adding details that answer **when, where, what, why,** or **how.**

Did you lose a **red, striped** hat, and is this yours**?**

Do you want to play **soccer with us,** or do you want to watch**?**

Add details to expand each compound interrogative sentence.

Sample answers are provided.

1. Should we go, or should we stay?

Should we go now, or should we stay longer?

2. Is Jade moving, or is she staying?

Is Jade moving to Texas, or is she staying in Maine?

3. Is Rebecca here, or is she home?

Is Rebecca here on the playground, or is she home?

4. Is that the last, or are there more?

Is that the last apple, or are there more in the box?

Conquer Grammar • Grade 1 • © Newmark Learning, LLC

Conquer Grammar • Grade 1 • © Newmark Learning, LLC